The Long Road Home

Emigration Australia

The Long Road Home

Copyright 2009 Emigration Australia

ISBN: 978-1-4452-7651-9

First Edition: January 2010

All rights reserved. No part of this publication may be reproduced, stored in a retrieval system, or transmitted, in any form or by means, electronic, mechanical, photocopying, recording or otherwise, without prior permission of the author(s). This also takes account of any future methods of the above means.

This book is sold subject to the condition that it shall not, by way of trade or otherwise, be lent, re-sold, hired out or otherwise circulated without the author(s) prior consent in any form of binding or cover other than that in which it is published and without similar condition including this condition being imposed on the subsequent purchaser.

This edition is produced by:

www.emigrationaustralia.com

TABLE OF CONTENTS

1. A CHILD'S STORY — 2
2. INTRODUCTION — 4
3. A BOY AND HIS DREAM — 7
4. A DREAM REALISED — 16
5. DEPARTURE — 22
6. A NEW 'HOME' — 26
7. GOODBYE OZ — 36
8. DETERMINATION TO RETURN — 41
9. APPLICATION & STRESS — 50
10. A NEW BEGINNING — 56
12. BACK 'HOME' — 64
13. THE TURNING TIDE — 78
14. CAIRNS. A DREAM SHATTERED — 84
15. MELTDOWN — 94
16. A LIFE TORN APART — 97
17. THE LAW IS AN ASS — 101
18. THE 'RETREAT'. PEACE! — 115

19. NEW LOVE	128
20. CONFUSION	135
21. THE WARMTH OF CHILDREN	150
22. ABSOLUTE DESOLATION	156
23. SOCIAL SERVICES. MADNESS	161
24. RESENTMENT	177
25. HEARTBREAK ONCE AGAIN	183
26. TRYING TO CARRY ON	190
27. A BETTER PLACE	193
28. A NEW PERSPECTIVE	204
29. THE TRUTH. AT LAST	212
30. LOOKING BACK	216
31. TRYING TO UNDERSTAND	221
32. LEARNING ONCE AGAIN	225
33. RECOVERY	228
34. CONCLUSION. WELL NEARLY	230
35. A CHILD'S STORY. EXPLANATION	233
36. A FINAL NOTE	237

To walk through its red deserts alone,
yet to walk these same deserts surrounded.

To touch the vast emptiness and feel nothing,
yet to touch again and feel everything.

To be surrounded by complete nothingness,
yet be enveloped by this nothingness.

To look toward the sunrise and see nothing,
yet to look again and see everything.

To look up at the vast blue and imagine little,
yet to look again and imagine all.

To sleep at night and hear silence,
yet to sleep again and hear everything.

To look up at the stars and feel so isolated,
yet to look again and feel so comforted.

To wake in the morning and feel such a void,
yet to wake again and be enriched by this void.

To feel all your senses so nullified,
yet feel all your senses come so alive.

****

A Child's Story
****

A hot summer's day on a Norfolk beach. A young carefree eight year old is playing amongst the surf, splashing about as if nothing else mattered.

His grandparents look at him from their vantage point sitting high in the sand dunes. They would often call 'Careful now love, don't go too deep'. Or, 'Come on love, come and get your ice cream'.

Of course the young man in question would often turn and say, 'Alright Nan, alright Pop, I'll be there in a minute'. Knowing full well that he would continue to play in the surf with little thought being given to anything else.

After all, the sea and its ever present mystery held his young mind as if in a trance. Nothing seemed to enter his youthfull mind except for the fish, crabs, and the endless wonder that was before him.

He had been fascinated by the sea for many years. Since his earliest memories the sea held a mysticism that was difficult to explain. Everything about it was indeed a miracle.

By this time he had collected many a sea shell, rock, and tiniest of crustaceans. But out of the corner of his eye he sees a rather strange object. A fish maybe, no this was no fish. A wonder of the deep, no this was different.

Upon further investigation he sees that it is an object that he does not recognise, at all. After some more rather tentative investigations he decides to pick it up.

He rushes up the beach, dripping wet and somewhat excited at his latest discovery to where his grandparents are sitting, surely as adults they will be able to tell him what it is?

His Nan and Pop rush to cover him with the warmth and comfort of a soft towel, but before they can do so, the young man in question breathlessly and excitedly asks his grandparents, 'Nan, Pop, what's this?

He expects an expert answer. He also expects any reply to

to make perfect sense. After all, his loving grandparents had always been wise and very methodical in all their respones.

But no, the only reply he gets is one of confusion, and to some extent, anticlimax. His Pop replies, 'It's a boomerang son. Now put it down and eat your sandwiches.' His Nan interjects with, 'And keep that towel wrapped around you love before you catch your death'.

He sits on the sand dune dazed and somewhat confused. 'What the hell is a 'Boomerang'? he asks himself. His understanding of this object is one of confusion, and in no small measure, mystery.

The Long Road Home

Introduction
****

My relationship with Australia has been one of immense ups and downs, I hope to be able to show you within this book just how much Australia, and its people have impacted on me, and to an extent, all those around me for many, many, years.

It would be unrealistic of me to think that this book will have any impact on your own migration plans and thoughts, but I hope that some of the information I have included you will find of use to you. Maybe in the not too distant future you will be able to take some comfort from the words I have written.

In many ways this book is going to be a very cathartic experience for me, emotional, traumatic, exciting, cruel, enlightening, and to some degree, extremely self-centered.

I do not for one minute expect that the words written here will have any great impact on you emotionally. After all, one person's emotions are as individual as the person themselves. So it would be foolish of me to expect that anything written here would have such an impact.

But I hope in some small measure to show you that the migration process, and the aftermath, is often fraught with dangers and emotions that you thought impossible before you started out on your migration journey.

I offer the words written as a form of open dialogue that will hopefully have the very smallest impact on your own lives. What I hope the impact of the words to be are simply that it will show you that you are not alone when you consider migration to Australia as a viable alternative to your life in the UK at the present time.

As you would have gathered from reading my website and hopefully the accompanying books, you can see that Australia has over the last twenty eight years been an integral part of my life, and to some extent ruled for the most part of. It has also to some extent ruled the lives of all those around me, for better or worse, I will let you be the judge of this.

Even now, as I am typing these words I am still confused as to what my future holds. All I know is that Australia will continue to play a massive part in my life, and those that come into contact with me.

At times this journey has been painful and extremely sad, but these are the times when you come to appreciate just what is truly important in life. I have come to a point in my life where I accept full responsibility for all of my actions over the past twenty eight years.

There is no getting away from the fact that at times my love affair with Australia has been to the detriment of my personal life. I would like to say that I wish I could change things, but unfortunately I cannot, no matter how hard I try.

However, that does not negate the fact that at times I wish I had done things differently, then maybe circumstances may have been different, not only for me, but for all those around me.

If I had done things differently then maybe, just maybe, the place I find myself in today would be totally different.

I have no idea if this would be better or worse scenario, I have no way of finding out. But what I do know is that the place I am in at the moment is a place that I am enjoying, and indeed relishing.

Having read the last few paragraphs it sounds as if I do not regret anything that has taken place in my life up to now, and in a way, I guess this is true. Because to regret certain scenarios and situations would be not only foolish, but also extremely naïve of me.

If my life had been any different up to this point I do not know if the projects I have embarked on with the website and books would have come to fruition. There is no way of knowing this. So in essence all I can do is carry on and try my best, and maybe by going ahead with these projects I can in some small way vindicate my actions, and hopefully make those around me see that each and every action I took was never intended to be cruel or vindictive in anyway.

Selfish maybe, but never did I go out of my way to be cruel or vindictive to all those around me. I hope by reading this book you can see what I trying to say.

The Long Road Home

A Boy And His Dream.
****

I was never what you would call 'academic', I enjoyed school immensely, maybe that was the problem, after all, are you really meant to enjoy school to the degree I did? Whilst I said I am not academic, I did try my very hardest in all of my lessons, well, at least the lessons I enjoyed.

I was like the vast majority of kids my age, playful, happy, and at times mischievous. However, I was never rude or belligerent, just at times a little cheeky that bordered on the farcical and ridiculous.

As with most of us we all have school lessons that we remember with fond memories. Memories that are as vivid today as they were many years ago. These memories that we hold so dear could be there for any number of reasons. Maybe it was a subject that we truly had a keen interest in. Maybe they were lessons that meant we could get to sit next to our best mate. Maybe, even lessons that meant we had the opportunity to interact with the opposite sex.

But my main reason for enjoying one particular subject at school was simply that it involved learning about the world, and was taught by a teacher by the name of Mr Baker. The subject was geography.

Now 'sir', as I will now refer to him was an inspiration to the whole class, particularly the boys. An inspiration for one reason and one reason alone. It was not the way he taught us, nor the language he used, or anything to do with his teaching technique. Having said this, sirs ability to teach in a manner that we all understood was without precedence, to say otherwise would not be doing sir justice.

No, the main reason we all looked forward to our geography lessons so much was the fact that sir was a former RAF pilot who flew Spitfires during the second world war.

He was to the vast majority of us a real hero, who had lived through a war not as a bystander, but an actual real life Spitfire pilot. A man whose courage and heroism was truly astonishing to his class of fourteen year olds who would look upon sir as not only an excellent teacher, but also a real live embodiment of all that was right and proper in the world we knew and lived through.

Whilst we all knew of his previous life through chinese whispers, and the cackle and rumour that flow through any school corridor, never once did sir actually tell any of us of his younger days. This only led to even more mysticism and magic. If sir was not prepared to talk of his life flying Spitfires, then surely it must have been a life full of high adventure and danger?

I dare say the reality of the situation was somewhat different. Flying a fighter airplane in the second world war was I have little doubt, a terrifying and frightening experience. Yes, there must have been times when the experience got the adrenaline pumping, but I would imagine the vast majority of the time these brave men were in real fear for their lives.

But, being only fourteen years old at the time our minds were full of ideas and notions of the lucky few who were fortunate enough to have dog fights in the skies above England, and if fortune was on their side they had the opportunity to shoot down the nasty German airman.

Sir was a generous men, who would go out of his way to make sure that the information he gave was taken in by his pupils and assimilated in order for us to learn. I never heard him raise his voice once, just a glance in the direction of the perpetrator who was messing about was enough to restore order to his lesson.

I guess because we knew of his history, the boys especially would show him the respect he so deserved, and any messing about by the boys was quickly stopped if we felt sir had seen and heard enough.

As I previously said, I enjoyed my geography lessons immensely, and it would be a lie to say that I didn't enjoy learning about other countries, cultures and customs, but, and I am still wracked with guilt to this day, I did have an ulterior motive for my keen interest.

From the age of seven I had been an avid fisherman. This stemmed from an initial introduction to fishing with my dad. He had taken me down to my local river one summer's day and had decided that we should go fishing.

Bearing in mind then, and to this day, my dad cannot abide fishing I am still a little perplexed as to why he did it. But now as I am a dad myself I can see just why he did it. As parents you do all kinds of things that you wouldn't normally do, but you do these things to make your children happy, that's all my dad did, tried to make me happy.

I honestly don't think my dad realises even to this day just what impact that day had on me when he took me down to my local river, it is a memory I hold dear, and if truth were known, a memory that I keep at the forefront of my mind.

Anyway, I digress somewhat. I was trying to explain my ulterior motive for enjoying my geography lessons so much. The fact of the matter is that even though my dad and myself only caught one tiny minnow that day, it set in motion a series of events that have led to this point in my life.

By the time I had reached the age of eleven my passion for angling was even more intense, at times even at this young age I could see that it was becoming an obsession. My best mate, Mark, and myself would every weekend take ourselves off (again, with dad's taxi service) to any number of lakes and rivers to try and catch any fish that was silly enough to accept our poor offerings of bait.

Myself and Mark would often talk of the far flung possibilities that lay within the fishing world. We would talk of little else apart from the exotic species that could be found throughout the world's rivers, lakes and oceans.

I can honestly say that we spoke of little else, except on occasion we would talk about girls, girls, and maybe girls again. I hope you can see where I am going with this.

My geography lessons, even though very enjoyable and educational, were also a means of finding out about other countries and the fish that were to be found swimming in said countries.

So sir, even though I know you have since past away I would like to pass on my sincerest apologies for my lack of honesty and integrity whilst I was in your lessons. I am sure you would agree though, that at the very least we learnt a lot from you, least of which was where the big fish were biting. Rest well sir, and thank you.

As I have previously said, myself and Mark were obsessive fishermen, there were a few others in our group who also enjoyed fishing, but not to the extent that myself and Mark did.

Each and every Thursday a weekly newspaper called 'Angling Times' was on the newsstands. Myself and Mark lived our lives around each Thursday. We would be the first in the queue at the newsagents in the morning to grab our copy of the fishermen's 'bible'. There wasn't an article, advert or editorial that we did not read with gusto and digest in the hope that some of the information written would eventually sink in to our thick heads.

There was one particular article one week that was to change the course of my life. It was a full two page centre spread in colour that went into great detail about the fish species, and types of fishing that were available in Australia.

To our small band of fishermen Australia was a place of wonderment and awe. No one really knew just what impact this article would have on me as a person, and secondly, as a fisherman.

The article went into great detail about the fish species that were available all around Australia, and even gave a comprehensive colour guide to the fish identification, and where they might be found. Myself and Mark could not believe our luck. Even though the words written bore little resemblance to what we did every weekend, we did our best to try and understand fishing in Australia.

There were exotic species that to us at that time might as well have been aliens from another planet. But all I could see was the vibrant colours and great fighting abilities of these fish.

Now bearing in mind that Mark was also an obsessive fisherman, the article seemed to go slightly over his head. Mark had more of the mindset of a carp fisherman. He didn't mind sitting on a riverbank for hours at a time waiting for that one 'big' fish. Whereas I didn't really mind what I caught, as long as it was a fish. As far as I was concerned the smallest of sticklebacks was indeed a fish that was worthy of interest and wonderment.

That's not to say I didn't enjoy my weekends camping out in all weathers looking for that one big fish, but I would have been quite as happy sitting on a riverbank catching small roach and minnows all day, just so long as it was a fish. To me, just to be able to look at an animal that comes from a realm that we understand little of was exciting and exhilarating beyond imagination.

The article in question was taken home with me and read incessantly each and every night until I had memorised every single word, and could recite them parrot fashion. In actual fact I remember buying a further two copies of the Angling Times so that I could keep at least one copy in pristine condition.

It is only now that I look back on that article and realise the impact it had on me. I very rarely stepped into my school library, unless of course I had yet again failed to do my homework on time and would try to find a quiet corner of the library where I could hopefully rush my homework and get it to the teacher on time.

But this one article had changed my life forever. The library now became my second home, where I would endeavour to find out as much as I could about Australia and its people.

When I say looking up everything to do with Australia what I really mean is that I would look up anything to do with

Australia, as long as somewhere within the text it mentioned fish and fishing, I know, shallow, maybe, but at the very least it was an 'education', of sorts.

I was as I have said only fourteen years old at this time so in essence I was living in a dreamland. Even though I learnt all I could about Australia and its fishing potential, I never, ever had any idea that one day I would end up there.

My school education carried on as normal, very rarely did it interfere with our fishing education. As was the norm, each and every weekend myself and Mark would find yet another lake or river to go fishing to.

Summer holidays were spent down at our local river with barely a day missed. We would rise at five in the morning and make our way down to the river in time for the sun to come up. Our summer holidays were basically orientated around where the fish were biting, and how we could catch them.

The months turned into years, and time as normal went on its merry way. Time was irrelevant to us, our only concern was that each and every weekend we would ensure that we had put into place plans, often of military proportions, for our next fishing adventure.

As time went by and we got older we came to realise that it was about time that we had to think about our long-term futures. Myself and Mark had made a pact many years before that when, and if a careers adviser came to our school we would both tell them that we wanted to be professional fishermen, and work on the trawlers.

Suffice to say that when a careers adviser did eventually come into our school and we suggested our long-term plans to him we were told to shut the door quietly behind us as we left. Looking back at that time I guess I can see why he said such a thing, but to not even be taken seriously is something that I find quite shocking, even to this day.

Yes, we were young, and I guess a little foolish. But our plans to work on a trawler were based on research and an understanding of the life involved. Maybe not a complete understanding, but nonetheless, an understanding that to a couple of fourteen year olds made commonsense, however misguided we may have been.

Anyway, life went on, and myself and Mark really had no idea what we wanted to do once we had left school. Bearing in mind that I was approaching sixteen at this stage, myself and my parents sat down and had some rather serious discussions about my future.

I had always liked the prospect of a career that had rules and regulations in place, and even at this early age I did have a huge pride in England. After many a long protracted conversation it was decided by us all that I would apply to the Royal Marines.

Even though my parents were extremely worried about my choice of career path they backed me to the hilt and told me that they would be extremely proud of me if I took such a path.

I have previously said that whilst not being particularly academic at school I always tried my best and would, most times give my all to whatever lesson was involved. So with this in mind myself and parents looked into the educational qualifications that were needed to facilitate entry into the marines. At this time the entry requirements were basically an all round education, and did not concern themselves with certain qualifications or academic attainment.

With this in mind, I left school with several CSE's, and on the whole I would say that I was a well rounded individual. Back in the early eighties many jobs were still open to people who did not obtain O and A-levels, so my CSE's would have been sufficient in any number of jobs.

As time went by I had become even more adamant in my decision to join the marines so I took myself off to Cambridge to the marine recruitment centre.

The centre was at that time a fairly relaxed and hospitable place. I met a sergeant there who talked me through my decision, and gave his experiences and advice in the hope that it would help me be sure that I was doing the right thing.

It was made plain to me that the life of a marine was at times, both physically and mentally demanding. It was not a life where you were molly coddled or cocooned in anyway, shape or form. At the conclusion of the interview I was still firm in my decision, and if it were at all possible, even more adamant to sign on the dotted line.

After this initial interview I was called back for a medical. This is where my life changed radically, at the time I thought for the worse, but looking back with the benefit of hindsight, it was for the better.

I did the basic physical exercises that are a pre-requisite for joining the marines, press ups, chin ups, and many other physical exercises that proved I was a worthy candidate to be considered for the marines.

The last test they gave me was one for colour blindness. Basically, it involved sitting in front of a computer screen and a simulated red and green flare would come from either side of the screen, it was my job to differentiate between the two as they merged together in the middle of the screen that lay before me.

I failed miserably. I had no problem at all when the flares were separate, but once they merged I could not differentiate between them at all. This was the first time I had been diagnosed with colour blindness, I couldn't believe it. I had passed the rest of the examinations with flying colours (sorry about the pun), but to fail on this really was a huge disappointment.

It was explained to me after this test that there was no way that I could progress any further. At the time I was extremely disappointed, and it showed. My dream of wearing the famous marine beret had been shattered, and now I was at a loss of what to do next.

I made my way home and told my parents of the news, the look on their faces were ones of disappointment, tinged with happiness. Disappointment for me, after all my dream now lay in tatters, but happiness in the fact that their son could no longer put his life in danger. I can look back at this time and understand exactly where they were coming from. At the time I was filled with a sense of huge disappointment, and in no small measure, failure.

I was truly dumbfounded, my plans and future had relied on being accepted by the marines, now that was not a possibility. What the hell was I going to do? I had absolutely no idea whatsoever.

Being the type of chap I am it didn't take me long to bounce back from this disappointment and once again look to the future, and hope in some small way to sort myself out. I have always been a rather optimistic character, and rarely will I let anything get me down. Or rather, let anything get me down in my younger years. I was in my future life to realise that at times, life really can make you feel as if it isn't worth carrying on.

A Dream Realised
****

The next stage of my life I remember as if it were yesterday. My dad was employed within the oil and gas industry. His job often meant him travelling overseas for extended periods of time, at times he would be away for six or eight weeks without coming home.

We had as a family become accustomed to this way of life. Since I was very young he had been employed in this particular field, and we were all used to him jetting off to another far flung destination on a regular basis. I very rarely saw my dad for any great length of time when I was younger, but this in no way was to the detriment of how close we all were.

It was just the 'norm' while I was growing up. Nothing unusual or out of the ordinary. We all thought little of it. However one particular day was to be different, and was to have an enormous impact on the rest of my life, and all those around me.

I remember my dad coming home one day and we were all sitting down in our living room and he announced that he was about to go overseas once again for the period of the year.

As was normal, we all sat around expectantly waiting to hear of his next destination. He had previously worked in Singapore, the Middle East, Malaysia, most of Europe and many other countries that I cannot recall right now, but at that time he had visited many an exotic and far flung destination.

We all thought that my father would be going back to one of these countries, as his expertise and skill was always in high demand throughout these parts of the world.

But to our amazement he announced that he had been offered a year's contract in Perth, Western Australia. For this reason alone during the next few paragraphs I am going to have great difficulty in trying to explain what impact this had on me.

Australia, a place that I had read about, heard about, and even seen on television. I had for the past three years eaten, slept and dreamt of little else. But more importantly, a place that meant fishing. I could lie to you and say that all that went through my mind were thoughts of seeing a new country, meeting a new people, enjoying their culture, seeing their sites, and for all intents and purposes, soaking myself in the atmosphere of a foreign land.

But all I had on my mind was the fishing that seemed to be so much better in this land called 'Australia'. A land on the other side of the world. A land where there were animals that were called 'Marsupials'. A land where the sun 'always' shined, and it 'never', ever rained.

After the initial surprise and astonishment had subsided amongst my family, the general chat about the length of contract, living conditions, schooling, etc, and when this event was going to take place was all that was being discussed.

But my father then proceeded to say that the contract allowed families to accompany him on a long-term basis. My mum who had at this time just about taken on board what my dad had said was gobsmacked at the prospect of moving to the other side of the world, even though it may be for only a year.

My fathers normal term of contract was that of 'single' status. Where no matter if you were married, or in a long-term relationship, the partners of those contracted to work overseas were expected to remain in the UK, that was just the way it was.

But on this occasion the rules had been relaxed somewhat. Because of the distance involved, and the length of contract, the company my father was going to work for had changed the terms of contract, and he was allowed to take up to four family members with him.

As you can imagine, those words were indeed a blessing to me. Or had I misread the situation so completely and utterly? Did this now mean that I too would be able to travel to Australia? Or was it more likely the case that just my mum and younger brother would be lucky enough to go?

It was at this point in time that my dad then proceeded to tell me that if I wanted to I could accompany them to Australia on the understanding that it may give me the opportunity to try and sort myself out, and come to a 'sensible' decision about my future.

However, all I could hear was, 'Andy, the fishing is great, why not come out for a year'. What my father was really saying was that as the contract was for a year it may give me sufficient time to come to a logical and educated decision about what I wanted to do.

There are very few people who know what impact this offer actually had on me then, and has had on my life to date. It was probably, no, indeed was, the biggest turning point in my life, and to date no other decision has ever influenced my life as much as this one.

I went to bed that evening with my mind full of expectations and dreams. In reality I truly had no idea what Australia had in store for me. After all, it was 1980, very few people from the UK had travelled to Australia for such an extended period of time, let alone maybe even a two or three week holiday.

I knew little of what Australia was about, to me it was just a country on the other side of the world that bore no relation to my life in the UK, and if truth were known, I had never thought I would be lucky enough to go.

But now I was faced with the possibility of travelling to Australia for an extended holiday, or so I thought. I don't think I slept a wink that night. My mind was full of pictures of Australia that had been burnt into my memory since that first glimpse of what Australia held in the Angling Times.

I had no real idea what Australia looked like, sounded like, smelt like, in fact, I truly was at a loss to try and describe in any great detail what Australia was going to be like.

My mind that evening was full of endless possibilities, most of which revolved around the potential fishing hotspots. Marlin, wahoo, tuna, the list was truly endless. All I could see in my minds eye was the fish species that were now going to ever so voluntarily throw themselves upon my fishing hook and succumb to a 'master angler'.

I now know that my parents would often talk long and hard about me travelling to Australia with them. I was after all, only seventeen years old. I dare say their conversations revolved around the fact that at seventeen I could have stayed in the UK along with my elder brother and looked after the house and got my nose to the grindstone and found work.

But in the cold light of day they knew I had no idea what I wanted to do, so it was agreed that I would go to Australia with them, in this way it would give me the chance to look long and hard at myself and decide what to do with my future.

Only now can I look back at this time and realise what a hard decision it must have been for my parents to make. Even though my father had on many occasions travelled extensively, he knew little of what Australia was like. My mother had no knowledge at all. So for them to agree for me to accompany them must have been a very hard decision for them to arrive at.

I awoke the next morning as excited as could be, the last time I felt like this was on Christmas Eve as a kid awaiting the arrival of Father Christmas, it really was the opportunity of a lifetime, and the excitement I felt knew no bounds.

That day I was like a cat on a hot tin roof, the expectation I felt was immense, and to this day I cannot remember feeling like this again. All I could think of was what lay ahead of me in terms of the fishing, after all, I was barely seventeen years old, and as I have said, obsessive about my fishing.

The following morning I went down to Mark's house and told him the news. Bearing in mind myself and Mark had been best mates for well over five years he took the news as I thought he would, with graciousness and generosity. He even said to me did I remember the article in the Angling Times, and did I still have it?

That day was filled with laughter and jokes. We both knew that Australia was a dream come true, and to be given the opportunity to travel there was indeed the chance of a lifetime.

There would be many other occasions that myself and

Mark would meet, but each and every time the conversation would eventually get around to Australia, and what we thought it may be like. I promised Mark on numerous occasions that I would, no matter what, keep him posted when I was out there and would at every available opportunity write to him.

To cut a long story short the lead up to the move was a very stressful time for all those involved, not least my mum and dad. My eldest brother, Pete, was going to stay in the UK, as he had a job that he enjoyed immensely with excellent prospects, and besides this, he was, and is, far more responsible than me, and he could be trusted to look after the house with care and attention.

My mum and dad were going to miss him immensely, but commonsense prevailed and we all agreed that Pete would stay in the UK and take care of things back here. My younger brother Martin, would also come out to Australia with us, so my parents also had the worry of finding schooling for him and making sure he was OK. He was only seven at the time, so it was only right and proper that he would be my parent's main concern.

It was a very emotional time for all those involved, and to say it put a strain on all of us would be an understatement. The mere fact that you have chosen to read this book I would imagine means you have a vested interest in trying to emigrate to Australia.

Bearing in mind that we were travelling to Australia purely on a visitors visa, with the exception of my father, does negate certain situations and circumstances arising from a formal application to emigrate. I was to find out how stressful and worrying the migration process was to be at a later date.

But having said this, our situation at the time was somewhat stressful on all those concerned, and some of the emotions we were to go through, though less painful, were still there for all to see.

Families still had to be told of our plans, goodbyes said, and plans made for our short-term future in Australia. Even though my dad's contract was only for a year, the emotions involved were at times nearly too much to bear, but had to be faced.

What must also be remembered was the fact that we were in the fortunate position that my fathers company were doing most of the arranging for us. They would source suitable accommodation, schooling for my younger brother, and for all intense and purposes, they took a lot of the responsibility off my parents shoulders.

The only thing that they could not take away was the emotional impact this move was to have on everyone involved, my grandparents, uncles, aunties, etc. We had always been a very close family, and it was going to be a huge wrench to walk away from this for a year. But it was something that had to be faced, and all of our responsibility to try and get through this somehow.

Rather selfishly during all of this time I had in the back of my mind the thoughts of what Australia was actually like. I had heard that it was hot, the beaches were gorgeous, and the wildlife wanted to kill you at every opportunity. As you can see, I truly had no concept of reality when I thought of Australia in those early days. This was going to change very, very soon as the arrival into Australia was imminent.

I was still only seventeen years old when this decision had been taken, so I can use as my 'defence' my age, inexperience and ability to ignore the bigger emotional aspects as it were. Looking back at these times I can see that I was young and naïve, and really had no idea what was involved in moving to the other side of the world.

Departure
****

Our tickets had been booked for the twenty eighth of May 1980, and it was all I could do to keep my excitement within reasonable bounds. All I knew was the fact that we were going to a country that held so many possibilities that it was nearly unbelievable.

Once we knew of the date of our departure I would like to say that things settled down a bit, but this could not have been further from the truth. My parents main concern was my elder brother, Pete. No matter how capable and responsible Pete was, it was evident, and rightly so, that my parents were going to worry about him no matter the assurances and promises.

Pete, as I have said, has always been far more responsible than me, and to me, seventeen years old, of course he could cope. He was my 'big brother', and was more than a match for anything that may crop up while we were away. After all, he had a long-term girlfriend who was as responsible as Pete, and I was sure that everything would be OK. My parents however thought otherwise. Not because they did not trust him, far from it. They were just doing what any responsible parents would do, and that was to worry.

Eventually the seconds, minutes, weeks and months gradually went by, and the very next day we were to depart for Australia. The other side of the world. An adventure. A new country that we would all learn to love!

The morning dawned like any other, with one massive difference, this was to be the day that would change my life, forever. There is no other way of putting it. This day in my life was going to change me drastically as a person, and to some extent, all those around me.

It is very difficult to convey just what took place on this day. People often say that there are certain scenarios in ones life that will change you as a person, for the rest of your life. This was to be one of those days. I have since had many different experiences throughout my life, and they have all had an impact on me, and made me the person I am today.

But this one day was to be a turning point in my life. A day that has since its very dawning influenced almost everything, and everyone around me, to a greater or lesser extent. It was a day that is burnt deep inside me, and a day that I have learned to love, and at times, hate.

My father was already in Australia, his work commitments dictated that he had to be in Australia whilst arrangements were made back in the UK. This would also give my dad the opportunity to make sure that everything was as it should be. The house his company had sourced was I dare say, cleaned on many occasions, as I know only too well that my dad would have wanted everything to be perfect for our arrival.

On the actual morning itself the goodbyes and tears were at times hard to bear. My mum who had a fantastic relationship with her parents found it extremely difficult to say goodbye, and vice versa. To say it was a difficult time for all those involved would be an understatement.

Our taxi was booked for ten thirty that morning and we waited with excitement and trepidation its arrival. My grandparents, uncles and aunties had all come over to our house to say their goodbyes, and if truth were known this made the whole situation ten times worse, but I guess we would not of had it any other way.

The journey to Heathrow airport was one of little consequence, except for the fact that we were to be away for a whole year, and not return until the next year. I was excited at the mere prospect of travelling to Australia. The thoughts and emotions I was feeling are inexplicable. They were thoughts of a world where everything was so different, the sun was always shining, and the people looked happy.

We boarded the 747 on time. Previously I had been on several school trips which involved an aircraft journey of some description. But in essence these school trips had only been to

Europe, and the flights involved very short indeed.

This was going to be a wholly different adventure. To me, the 747 aircraft was more akin to a medium sized building. I could not believe the size and mass of the bloody thing. It was immense. To this day I still find it amazing that one of these airplanes can actually take off, remain in the air, and safely disgorge its passengers at the other end.

It truly was a massive. My mum, Martin and myself boarded the aircraft with a sense of excitement and trepidation. My father was in Perth awaiting our arrival, so it was down to my mum to make sure we were all OK.

Bearing in mind that she had travelled quite a bit, I still think the journey that lay before her filled her with dread and fear. Martin and I just found the whole experience very exciting, if truth were known, I found the whole experience one that I will always remember, Martin was after all only seven years old, so a lot of what was going on went over his head somewhat.

We sat down in our seats and tried our best to prepare ourselves for what lay ahead. All and sundry will tell you that Australia is a long, long way away, but it is not until you board an aircraft and actually fly to Australia that you realise just how far it really is.

Twenty one hours spent on an aircraft is a very long time. Being only seventeen years old I could cope with this far better than my mum, who found the whole experience both tortuous and extremely draining. I remember looking at my mum on several occasions and she looked absolutely awful, she will forgive me my comments, as I think she would agree that any journey to Australia was, and is, for her a hell on earth.

This is where I discovered an attribute of mine that had laid dormant up to this point in time. Within the space of one hour I was beginning to feel very drowsy indeed. It was all I could do to keep my eyes open for any length of time.

Maybe it was the noise of the aircraft. Or it may have been the ever so slight motion of the aircraft, but all I knew was that all

I wanted to do was go to sleep and rest. But whilst I may of only been seventeen years old, I still had a keen sense of responsibility toward my mum and younger brother.

It fell upon me to make sure that they were both looked after, and I realised that it was down to me to make sure this happened. I would like to say that I lived up to my responsibilities very well, but in actual fact I slept for the vast majority of the time.

I occasionally woke up, when nudged by my mum to partake of the meals that were brought around, but within minutes of consuming the said meal I was well and truly asleep once again.

It is a facet of my nature that I still have this ability to fall asleep on any aircraft. I have been backwards and forwards many times not only to Australia, but many other countries, and I still manage to fall asleep in the vast majority of cases.

People that I am close to will rarely admit it, but it is one side of my character that they find extremely annoying. After all, my poor travelling companions are often the ones where they find it impossible to sleep for any amount of time, and for them to turn to me and see me fast asleep must be truly annoying.

As I said, very few of those that I have travelled with will admit it, but at times I would imagine that they want to stab me in the cranium with one of the plastic knives that the airlines provide.

After some fourteen hours the plane stopped off in Kuala Lumpur for the mandatory refueling and cleaning. This pit stop was barely three hours long, and all of the passengers had to disembark the aircraft for the necessities to be carried out. All I will tell you at this point in time is that the heat we experienced in Kuala Lumpur was immense, and we were later to learn that we would have to endure this heat on a daily basis in just over a years time.

A New 'Home'
****

As we approached Western Australia on our flight path it was all I could do to stem my excitement. The approach of the Jumbo took us across the Indian Ocean, as blue and as iridescent as I had imagined, if not more so. Even though my mum was sitting in the window seat I still managed to extend my neck as far as I could, and look out of the tiny porthole.

I could of sworn I saw sharks, marlin, wahoo, all swimming in the deep blue. My imagination was playing tricks on me, but at that time I was adamant in what I thought I saw.

The outline of the coast soon came into view. Australia, a country I had dreamt about for many years was now in sight. It is completely impossible to put into words how I felt at this time. I have never felt the same way again about anything in my life.

We arrived in Perth on a bright May afternoon, of course we had flown out of the UK in the summer, but this was Australia's winter, not that you would know, it was still very, very mild, and the sun was high in the sky. The journey had been long, and at times extremely boring, well at least for those poor souls that hadn't slept.

After we disembarked the plane we then approached the customs hall where we were to be given the all clear to enter Australia, officially. I have to this day several items in my possession that I hold dear. Of course the people in my life that I care about and love will always remain my greatest pleasure, but there are certain inanimate objects that I possess that mean an awful lot to me.

This was going to be one of those occasions. It was the briefest of experiences, but it did lead to a significant moment in my life. After a very brief, but courteous conversation with the customs official he very kindly placed a stamp in my passport.

There, as bold as brass was the official welcome to Australia. I still have this original stamp to this day, and it is looked upon with a sense of wonder, and at times, great affection.

After clearing customs and baggage claim we then proceeded to walk through immigration and hopefully find my dad on the other side. My mum at this time felt absolutely terrible, she suffered terribly from migraines at the best of times, and this journey had really taken its toll on her.

All I remember is my dad waiting on the other side of the barriers with a huge grin on his face, unfortunately my mum did not return the favour, and if I remember correctly she said 'Don't you ever make me do that journey again'.

It is only now that I can see what my mum meant, at the time I thought it a rather vicious and negative comment. After all, my dad had given us all the opportunity of a lifetime, and surely we should all be grateful for this? But no, my mum really was absolutely raving mad with my dad for making her travel such a long way, and she was now on the other side of the world many thousands of miles away from her family and home.

Having got older, and experienced exactly what she did, I can now see her point of view exactly, but at the time I thought it a rather negative and hurtful statement to make. God only knows how my father felt? His world must of imploded, ever so slightly. But I have to give him his due, not once did he show it. He just continued to smile and ask all of us if we were OK?

The journey from the airport to the house my dad had rented took approximately forty five minutes, it was early afternoon and this gave me the opportunity to look around me, and now at last I could get a clear picture of what Australia looked like, sounded like, and smelt like. My senses were bombarded with absolute shock and awe. This was nothing like England. I don't know what I had expected, but I certainly hadn't expected this.

It was so new, nothing seemed of any great age, everything just looked so new. Nothing it is seemed was even vaguely familiar, absolutely nothing reminded me of 'home'. The sights and smells that greeted me were unprecedented. The sun seemed to put a whole new complexion on everything that I saw.

This was certainly not England. This was a new country, and boy, did it seem like one.

To this day I do not know what I had expected, but it wasn't this. To me Australia had always been a dream, a dream that was never going to be fulfilled up until a few short months ago. Now that I was here I was dumbfounded as to what lay before me.

My imagination up to this point had played all manner of tricks on me. I would often sit up in bed back in the UK and try to somehow teleport myself into Australia to see what was awaiting me. But not in my wildest imagination could I have possibly seen this.

Even then, when I was only seventeen years old and had only experienced Australia for no more than thirty minutes I knew that this was a place I was going to be extremely happy in. I cannot put my finger on it, I have tried to take myself back to that time and ask myself what went through my mind that made me so sure that this was going to be a place that would remain with me to my dying day?

As I said, I cannot put my finger on it, but Perth just seemed to welcome me, and I know this is going to sound too deep for some, but it was the first time I had felt emotionally connected to a country. Obviously, I had always been connected to the UK, but this was mainly due to the friends I had, the family I had around me, the people I knew and loved.

This was different, this was a country, an inanimate object that for all intents and purposes was just that, an inanimate object made out of concrete, steel and plastic. Things that do not live or breath, they are just the structural basis that any city is built upon. Surely it is the people that give a country it's real personality? But this was different. Perth did feel as if it had a personality, a personality that was welcoming, friendly, and only too pleased to welcome a young lad by the name of Andy into its fold.

As I said, some people may find these thoughts a little too deep, and even a bit 'airy fairy'. But I find it nearly impossible to explain just how I felt. The only way I may be able to explain it is we all know the feeling of when we walk into a house, or any new location, and we immediately feel at home there. None of us can put our finger on it, but the place we are in seems to envelop us and enchant us in a way that we have rarely felt before.

I have tried over the years to try and put my finger on it, without success may I add. After all, the only people I had met in Australia up to this point were the customs officials and immigration staff. Whilst they were extremely friendly and affable you could not say by any stretch of the imagination that they influenced my thoughts and emotions to any great deal at this time.

Perth just seemed to welcome me, to make me feel immediately at home, and in some way say to me that Australia was indeed a very special place, and would remain with me until the present day, and hopefully forever more.

Perth was loud, brash and so new. But I had the feeling that deep down it had a kind and welcoming soul. The sun was blazing, the pavement actually shone in its shadow, and the whole city seemed to be so very proud of itself. As I said, an inanimate object, maybe. But to me Perth had found a place within me that remains with me to this day.

We arrived at our rented property some forty five minutes later, to me, it was just a house, very nice and looked comfortable, but it was still just a house at the end of the day. To my mum this was going to be her home for the next year, and the look on her face was one of disappointment, and to some extent, absolute rage.

She had been used to her home in the UK, her surroundings had been built up over many years, and she had made it a warm and loving home for all of us, to this day it is a house that when I am back in the UK I still call 'home'. Even though my parents have moved on several occasions since this time, I still look upon the house in Hertfordshire as my home.

To her, Australia was as alien as anything you could

imagine. None of the familiar surrounds, very few of the people she loved and cared about, and most of all I dare say her mind was still in the UK thinking about Pete, and all of her relatives and friends. My mum at this time was the unhappiest I had ever seen her, but I hoped that one day she would accept Australia in some small way.

The new house to her was so vastly different to the one she had left behind in England. Our new home was very modern, open plan, and extremely bare of what she would call 'character'.

I guess what I could not understand was that she did not seem to except Australia as I had done, even though we had only been in the country for less than two hours. I couldn't understand how she could not see Australia as I did, it took a long time for me to understand my mums behaviour, and now I can see with hindsight the impact it must have had on her.

As I said, the house was just that, somewhere where I would eat and sleep with a roof over my head and my family would be safe, but that is as far as it went. Within fifteen minutes of entering the front door I was pestering my dad to find out where the nearest newsagents was. All I wanted to do was find out where the nearest newsagents was and buy as many fishing magazines as I possibly could, that was all that was on my mind.

You can imagine the dilemma facing my father. He had just introduced most of his family to Australia, and the reaction he had received from my mum was somewhat negative. He also had the worry of my younger brother, who by this time was rather tearful and bordering on the hysterical. After all, he was only seven years old and the whole journey was beginning to take its toll on him.

And there was me, making a complete pain of myself and pestering him for information that I would imagine he had little knowledge of, or indeed, interest in. I think more in frustration than love my father informed me where I should go! My dad explained to me that it was just over the road, about a five minute walk.

My parents were rather concerned that I had arrived in a new country and was going to rush out across the road to buy a few magazines. Now that I am a parent I can see that if my seventeen year old son or daughter said such thing I would worry beyond belief, and be concerned for their welfare.

But I was adamant in my opinion, I had rough directions and off I went. My dad had said it was a shopping mall, a shopping mall I asked myself, what the hell was that? As I proceeded down the road I was expecting to see a row of shops on the high street with something resembling WH Smith's as the newsagent. But no, what lay before me was a complete shock.

The shopping mall in question was gigantic, absolutely astounding and huge. Now I could see why my parents were so worried. Now that I am an adult I can put this into context. Garden City was in fact roughly the size of three or four football pitches, to a young lad who was used to an English high street this came as a complete shock.

The car park itself was the size of a football pitch, and cars were parked row upon row upon row. I entered through the side entrance and there before me stood department stores, all manner of speciality shops that at that time, took my breath away. I could not get over the size of the interior, there was even music playing in the background, and God forbid, several coffeehouses were housed within this massive structure.

This was a completely alien and new to me. I had been used to an English high street where there were rows of small independent shops lining the streets, all carefully arranged in some kind of order. Here, in Perth, was a shopping mall the like of which I had never seen. The shops were big and brash, bright and in your face. It took me a while to assimilate this information and to gather my thoughts.

It even smelt different. New, clean, and if truth were known, rather sterile. But I liked it. To me it seemed as new as a shiny tack. It was a place that I felt immediately at home in.

And the people. I couldn't get over the differences. The

vast majority were wearing shorts and t-shirts. I had come out to Australia in the early winter and so the vast majority of people were dressed accordingly. Casually, some would say, rather unkempt I thought at first glance. They did not seem to have the same demeanour as my brethren back in England. They were very, very different.

Once I had got my breath back I decided that the best course of action was to just walk and hopefully I would eventually come across a bookstore or newsagent that would hold what I was looking for.

I wandered for what seemed like an eternity. Staring, looking, at times in utter bemusement at what lay before me. I must of stared at certain people for some time, it still surprises me to this day that I didn't get a mouthful of abuse from someone.

It took a while to get my bearings, but eventually I could see at the end of the complex a newsagent housed within a department store. This I hoped would be the answer to my dreams. Fishing magazines that would back up every thought and emotion I had about the endless fishing possibilities in Australia.

I went into the newsagent full of anticipation and eagerness. I cannot put into words just what this moment meant to me. And there before my eyes were rows upon rows of magazines concerning all matters Australia, but most importantly, several shelves were dedicated to Australian fishing, and the species of fish found therein.

I was like a kid in a sweet shop. To try and encapsulate just how I felt is very nearly impossible. I had been an obsessive fisherman since I was seven years old, and I had been obsessive about Australian fish since the age of fourteen, and now I was faced with a plethora of books that dealt specifically with all things fishy in Australia.

I didn't know which way to turn first, my mind was racing, my palms sweaty, and my heart rate must have doubled in intensity. I know it will come across as rather ridiculous now to a bystander, but the emotion and thoughts I had then were intense indeed.

The first book I picked up was around four inches thick and was titled 'The Australian Fishing Encyclopedia'. My fingers could not turn the pages quickly enough. I had read about, and seen many of the species that were detailed in this book, and now to be faced with so much detailed information was nearly more than I could bear. I will not bore you with the information that was enclosed, I know only too well that many non-fishermen have become bored very quickly if I go into too much detail.

The only way I can explain how I felt is this. If you could magnify how you felt on Christmas Eve when you were a child in the UK one hundred fold, then you may come somewhere near feeling as I did at that time.

As we get older there are very few things in life that truly excite us and make our heart miss a beat, but this was one of those instances. To this day I relive it time and time again, it still brings back many happy memories.

Unfortunately as we do get older these sort of emotions can pale into the background because of the worries and troubles we have as fully grown adults, we at times seem to have the weight of the world upon our shoulders, and for this reason it is hard to have such feelings as we did when we were children, it's a shame, but nonetheless true.

I spent nearly two hours in that bookstore, even this wasn't long enough, but I knew my parents would be worried if I did not return home fairly soon. My dad had given me a couple of dollars to spend, so I eagerly bought 'The Australian Fishing Encyclopedia' and made my way back to our new house.

By this time I had calmed down somewhat, and it was at this time the reality of my new life begun to sink in. The initial journey to the shopping mall had been somewhat of a haze. After all, I had only one thing on my mind at that time, fishing magazines. Now that I had the opportunity to collect my thoughts somewhat it began to dawn on me just what lay before me.

As I walked home I began to take in far more than I had

originally done so. Even the roads were different. Not the normal small highways of England. Now I had to negotiate a road that was six lanes wide and full of speeding traffic. The cars were out of this world, bigger, brighter and faster.

There was no real grass to speak of. True, it was greenish in appearance, but it was so different. Coarse underfoot, it crunched as you stepped on it. It was also interspersed with sand. Sand I said to myself, what the hell was this all about? The houses were a complete contrast to what I had been used to. They were so much bigger, and much more brash. I tried to take all of this in, but fell short somewhat, and it was only after some time that I would begin to understand what had taken place.

When I arrived home once again I remember seeing my mum fast asleep on the living room couch, she did look terrible, tired and very, very fraught. My dad, who had obviously, as ever done his best, looked sorely disappointed that my mum felt as she did. I guess it was a mixture of disappointment and utter worry, he was always used to my mum being strong for all of us, and in control of every situation.

Now, my mum just looked very tired, and I dare say my dad thought that she may want to return to the UK as soon as possible, in actual fact he wasn't far off the mark, what transpired later would make us all look at Australia in a different light. My younger brother at this time was also fast asleep in the armchair, it had all been too much for him, and he basically fell asleep through utter exhaustion.

I too was feeling somewhat tired by this stage, but the sheer excitement of being in Australia kept me going, and I also realised that my father would need some help to get things sorted so that we could all try to settle in far quicker.

That weekend was what you could call somewhat tense. I don't think that my parents spoke to each other at any great length. My mum was still feeling the after effects of the flight, and she knew that on the following Monday my younger brother would have to go to a new school. So her main concern was that of Martin and his welfare.

Monday morning soon came around and it was obvious that even though my mum, and to an extent my younger brother Martin needed my dad around it was obvious that he had to go to work for the sake of all of us. This was met with a somewhat negative attitude by my mum, but it was obvious that this was a path that had to be taken.

To me at this time Australia was exceeding beyond a doubt every expectation and dream I had of it. Australia in my opinion just got better and better. I remember showing my mum and younger brother where the shopping mall was, and each and every time I walked out of the front door Australia was there to welcome and embrace me.

I couldn't get over how very different it was. This country was so vastly different to the one I had left behind. Nothing, absolutely nothing was familiar. Even the sky looked completely different, and for all intents and purposes I could have been on another planet. The first few weeks spent in Perth have proven to be a milestone in my life.

Goodbye Oz
****

After several weeks a routine was soon slipped into. My father would go to work, my younger brother would get the school bus, and it was left down to myself and mum to try and find our way around. By this time I was becoming more and more fond of our new home, I could find little to complain about. My mum on the other hand hated every waking minute of her new life.

The heat, flies, food, TV, people, weather, all seemed to take their toll on her, in fact she could not adapt at all. She was used to having her familiar things around her. She had made a wonderful home back in the UK for all of us, and to say she missed it would be a gross understatement. And of course she was missing my elder brother very much. It was as if she was not complete. The worry and anxiety she felt I can only now come anywhere near appreciating.

I will not bore you with my fishing escapades. Suffice to say that each and every weekend my dad, bless him, would take me to the nearest stretch of coastline so that I could go fishing. Never once did he complain. I think he realised that I wouldn't take no for an answer, and in all probability he was only too keen for me to get out of the house as the atmosphere at times in the family home was rather tense.

The fishing lived up to all my expectations, and then some. Whilst it took me a while to get into the swing of things I did eventually find a way of catching fish on a regular basis. However, what was surprising at that time, and still surprises me to this day is simply this.

That whilst I was an obsessive fisherman I found my interest waning somewhat. Waning for a rather strange and inexplicable reason. Australia to me had become a place that was truly magical in most aspects. It was so different to what I had been used to in England.

It gave me a freedom to be myself. Now that sounds a

rather strange and deep comment to make, but Australia and its people had stirred something in me that up until this point had lain dormant. I find it very difficult to explain this feeling, but it was a feeling that I had arrived somewhere that excepted me, but more to the point, didn't expect anything of me.

It was a feeling of welcoming that I have not experienced anywhere else I have been to. That no matter what I did, Australia was now my home, or so I thought. I found everything about the country exciting and enthralling.

Bearing in mind that I was now approaching eighteen years of age you would of thought that my interests lay elsewhere, but in point of fact I did all I could to try and learn as much as I could about this country, and the people that lived there.

From the flora and fauna, which still fascinate me to this day, I found a constant source of inspiration. The outback, its vast nothingness intrigued me no end. The history of this great country was to me, astounding. I even became somewhat of a history buff and learnt all I could about the early settlers too Australia. I had maps and books which went into great detail about every aspect of Australia and its people. I had for all intense and purposes fallen in love with this country, and wanted to learn more and more about it.

Australia had cast a spell on me, as far as I was concerned this was going to be the place where my future lay. I had little doubt that Australia would be with me forever, and I was going to do whatever was required to enable this to happen. Or at least I thought so.

I had kept myself very busy during the first nine months of our stay in Australia. I had done all I could to help my mum out around the house and with the day to day chores that are involved in any life. Even though I had done all I could it was blatantly obvious that my mum was never truly going to settle.

To her Australia was as alien now as it had been when she first stepped off the airplane. She did however except Australia to some extent after we moved houses. We moved to an area of

Perth that was a much older suburb. Once there she seemed to be a bit happier, thankfully.

We all knew the time would come when my fathers contract would expire and it was a day I was dreading. After all, I had now wholeheartedly excepted Australia as my new home and I was going to move hell and high water to stay here.

Unfortunately at that time the immigration authorities had little sympathy with an eighteen year old who saw Australia as his new home. The immigration rules and regulations at this time were mainly based around a point scoring system, much as it is today.

However, looking back at this time, the points system was easier to understand, and did to a certain extent allow a broader spectrum of people to apply for visas, it still wasn't easy, but nonetheless, a little less stringent.

I had done as much research as I possibly could. While my age may have been a positive when looked at within the immigration criteria, I had little else going for me. No qualifications to speak of, well at least none that were recognised in Australia, very little money, and lets face it, what was I going to contribute to Australia, except my passion for the country.

The day finally dawned when my father said to all of us that his contract was about to expire, and we would all have to start to think about the future.

I had come to love Perth, and Australia as a whole. I was approaching eighteen and as is the norm with most stroppy teenagers they think they know it all, I was no exception to the rule. There were times when I realised that I had little choice but to go back to the UK and I took it out on my mum and dad.

As a family we did however speak seriously of me trying to stay in Australia. We looked at most avenues that may be open to me, but this was to no avail. The immigration policy was then, as it is now, extremely complex, and it is not just a matter of letting anybody into Australia.

So in essence, the avenues that we investigated would

never can come to fruition, but that never stopped me looking at every possibility that was available, but in the end I was left with little choice but to return to the UK with my family.

That makes it sound as if I never wanted to return to the UK with my family, nothing could be further from the truth. It was just that now Australia had become part of me, it had managed to invade my every thought, night and day, and in some way managed to get hold of me like nothing else had before.

To try and put this feeling into words is nearly impossible. How on earth can a country get this type of hold on you, and the longer you stay in the country the hold just gets tighter and tighter? Australia to me at this time was the country that I looked upon as my home, even at this young age I realised that Australia was the country I wanted to make my future in.

However hard it was to accept, the day finally dawned when we all had to depart for the UK, very few people know this, but it was one of the saddest days of my life. To say goodbye to a country that had been so good to me was gut wrenchingly sickening.

Australia and its people, even though I had only experienced them for less than a year, had truly left their mark on me, and when you have to say goodbye to such a place, and a people, it is indeed very hard.

However, there was one difference this time. Instead of flying directly back to the UK my father announced that he had been offered a job placement in Kuala Lumpur, Malaysia. This came as a complete surprise to all of us, not least my mother. She had after all been looking forward to getting back to her home and seeing her family, relatives and friends once again.

This contract too was one that allowed my father to take his family along with him, and was an option that he put to all of us. Now bearing in mind my mothers attitude to being away from her home for any length of time her response was somewhat surprising. Without hesitation she said that we would all travel to Malaysia with my father and make the most of this opportunity.

To this day I still find it difficult to fathom her reasoning. Maybe it was just simply the fact that she was going to get out of Australia, or maybe it was more of the attitude of 'in for a penny in for a pound'. I still do not know why she had come to the conclusion she did, but I am glad she did so.

As the days went by we all came to realise that our next adventure was only just around the corner. Whilst I would be lying to you if I said I was not looking forward to this next chapter in my life it was somewhat negated by the fact that I would have to say goodbye to a country that I truly loved and admired.

I was still of the opinion that Australia was my home and it was going to be heartbreaking to leave it. I had adapted brilliantly to my new surroundings, and I could not ever see myself making a home back in the UK.

The day finally dawned when we had to leave Perth. To this day it fills me with sadness and regret. But the one overriding thought that was in my mind was simply this. That one day I would return to Australia and make it my home. I had no idea about how I would go about doing this, but I was sure that it would happen. I would do everything in my power to ensure this was the case.

We all boarded the aircraft that May morning with a sense of excitement and anticipation. I however was of a slightly different mindset. I cannot possibly convey to you how I felt. Sad, hollow, empty, all manner of emotions were going through my mind. I remember vividly hearing and feeling the wheels of the aircraft leave Perth airports tarmac. Tears streamed from my eyes, and a complete and utter feeling of emptiness filled my very soul.

But the one thought that kept me sane was merely that one day I knew I would return. One day, whenever that may be. I knew not how, or when. But as I looked at the ever smaller ground beneath me I made a promise to myself that one day I would return and make a new life for myself in this wonderful country.

Determination To Return
****

I could go into great detail here about our time in Malaysia. But this book concerns itself with Australia and what it means to me. But suffice to say that during our three months in Malaysia we all had some great times and visited many other parts of south east asia. These adventures have made me into the person I am today, and I am truly thankful for that.

As I have said, this book is meant to chronicle my affair with Australia, so that is the tenure I shall keep to. But to try and convey some of my thoughts I will simply say this. No matter where I was, or who I was with, there was not one day that I did not envisage myself returning to Australia for good. This one thought kept me going, and it is a thought that has stayed with me till this day.

When we finally arrived back in England it goes without saying that my family and friends were over the moon to see us back, the relief on my mum was huge, she was finally back in the place she knew well and loved so much. She was amongst her family once again, and at last, she had a genuine smile back on her face.

She had smiled previously in Australia, but deep down you could tell there was deep unhappiness there. If there was one reason I was happy to be back in the UK it was for my mum, as I hated to see her how she was in Australia the vast majority of the time.

After the initial hugs and kisses from all those concerned it was amazing how quickly things settled down and we got into a routine. At times it was as if we had never been away for any length of time. My father had found a new contract in London, my brother's career was going well, and my younger brother Martin had started school. But I still truly had no idea what I wanted to do, with one caveat.

I was determined to get back to Australia as soon as possible. I had no idea how I was going to do this, but I knew deep down that there must be a way of returning to Australia, no matter the price I had to pay. I had just turned eighteen and what you could call very, very determined, so each and every waking moment I was going to do all I could to find out if a return to Australia was a viable possibility.

Of course then the internet was in its infancy, so to find out information was slightly more difficult than it is in this day and age, but there were still libraries, telephones, and fax facilities that enabled me to find out the relevant information.

There were several possibilities that may have been open to me. But after further investigation it was obvious that only one of these avenues offered any hope of a realistic return to Australia. The most viable route was as an 'independent' applicant which took into account my age, english speaking ability and employment history.

Two out of these three prerequisites were easily overcome. I was still young, and I could speak english well. The one hurdle that I had to overcome was my employment history. I had to be able to prove to the immigration authorities that I had a trade or skill that would be in demand in Australia.

You could hardly call my fishing career and interest in all things fishy a 'trade' by any stretch of the imagination. So this was a hurdle that had to be looked at long and hard if my dream of living in Australia was going to become a reality. I needed to do some serious thinking, and quickly decided that I needed to get a trade in order for me to gain enough points that were a necessity to emigrate to Australia.

As I have said, I am not very academic. I am far from stupid, but I can be somewhat lazy in any field that doesn't really interest me. So, not being particularly academic I decided that the best path to take would be to get a trade within the building industry.

At that time, in the early eighties, there were several courses that I could have enrolled on, but after much deliberation and thought I decided to enroll in the local building college and take four modules in City and Guilds certification in carpentry and joinery, cabinet making, machine woodworking and general building construction.

I had done hours of research on this matter, and it was hoped that if I was successful in my future endeavours to gain the appropriate City and Guilds certification, then this combined with my age, language ability, and other attributes would meet all the requirements that were needed to enter Australia in the skilled visa program.

By this time I had once again met up with my good friend Andy, it was as if we had never been apart, we still had the same interests and goals, and our relationship continued from where it had left off. We still went fishing every single weekend, and all we ever seemed to talk about was fishing.

Andy was very similar to me in the fact that he didn't really know what he wanted to do with his future, so being the best of mates he decided that he would enroll on the same course as I was taking, and hopefully this would give him the future he wanted. As you would imagine I was over the moon at this prospect, Andy was my best friend, and it meant that the long bus journey to and from Colchester would not only be more pleasurable, but filled with laughter all the way.

Please bear in mind one point. Whilst I was excited and sure in my own mind that my future qualifications would enable me to go back to Australia I was to some extent living in a fools paradise.

Firstly, there was the fact that though I was sure I would pass the exams with flying colours, this was in no way a certainty. I may indeed have failed them miserably, and it would have been four years wasted. Worse than this was the fact that if I did fail my exams then the immigration authorities would in no way even consider me as a suitable candidate.

Secondly was the fact that four years is a long time. For all I knew was that the immigration department may well change its entry requirements in this time frame. As is the case now, the immigration rules and regulations are in a constant state of flux, and to try to second guess the Australian immigration authorities is indeed foolish in the extreme.

I won't go into too much detail of how my time at college went. It was filled with laughter and jollity. Of course we learnt a lot, and all in all I had a great time at college. It wasn't all plain sailing, we did have our run ins with some of the staff and fellow pupils, but all in all it was a great four years and we enjoyed our time immensely.

At the end of the four modules myself and Andy were pleased to be told that we had passed, I cannot remember what Andy achieved, but I had received two distinctions and two credits which I must admit, I thoroughly deserved.

It must be said that during the four years of study at Colchester I had constantly been checking on the entry criteria of the immigration authorities. We all know that at times the criteria can change overnight and can put a great deal of stress on any applicant. So you can imagine being only eighteen I was at times desperate to make sure my qualifications would enable me to return to Australia, and its people.

At times the speed of such changes can be frightening, and it is all you can do to keep your sanity while the Australian immigration authorities debate over what is required to enter their country.

After all, even though I enjoyed myself immensely at building college the ultimate goal was to achieve sufficient qualifications that would satisfy the immigration authorities and show them that I was a suitable candidate to enter Australia on a permanent basis.

To say that it was a worrying time would be an understatement, there were times when I truly did not know if all the hard work and effort I put in would be worthwhile in the end.

The immigration policy was, and is, completely out of my control, little I said or did would have any influence on such matters. So I had to rely on the commonsense attitude of the immigration authorities, and hope that the avenue I was going down was going to be an avenue that would lead to a positive outcome.

My initial intention was to gain my qualifications, and then get an apprenticeship with a building company where I could work for two or three years in my chosen trade. This would then bolster my application to the immigration authorities. In those days apprenticeships were looked upon as very relevant to any long-term future in England, and if I could gain three years experience with a building company it would also give me more points needed when I finally applied to emigrate to Australia.

However, as with such things my timing was what you could call diabolical. It was now 1984 and the UK literally fell into a black hole. I understand a little of what went on, but to say I am expert in the field would be an over exaggeration. All I know is that within the space of six months I was made redundant three times, twice from local building contractors, and once from a London based company.

This was no one's fault, it was just a sign of the times, but unfortunately it had come at completely the wrong time for me. My plans had been set in concrete, I had just given four years of my life in order to get back to Australia, I had literally put my life on hold so that a return to Australia was a possibility, now all of my hard work and effort seemed to be in vain, and it was all I could do to keep my sanity.

Whilst I lost three jobs, I was fairly lucky in the fact that I still managed to find work, admittedly after some time, but at least it was work in my chosen trade.

At all times, even when faced with the prospect of redundancy yet again I had my goals fixed securely on the target of getting back to Australia. Yes, times were hard, and at times, very bleak. But I was still young and skilled and sooner or later things would turn around and I would once again be able to return to Australia.

It was at this point in time that Andy introduced me to a

young lady by the name of Jennie. I had several girlfriends in the past, but this was different, in some way I knew this was for the long-term. Myself and Jennie would see each other on a fairly regular basis, and things seemed to progress very well indeed.

As I said, my plans had been set in concrete, but as with most things in life things can change very quickly. Myself and Jennie were now getting very serious and eighteen months later we were married. It was one of the happiest days of my life when spoken in terms of human relationships, and we were as happy as the proverbial 'Larry'.

I had always been totally honest with Jennie throughout our relationship, and she knew of my plans to return to Australia, it goes without saying that now myself and Jennie were married, if she agreed, we would go to Australia as a couple.

By this time we were finding our budget extremely difficult to manage. We had bought a flat in a small village, we both had full time jobs, and we had not mortgaged ourselves up to the hilt. But the economic climate at that time really went insane, and our mortgage repayments went up by significantly within the space of several months.

The building trade had taken a huge hit, and I was finding it more and more difficult to find and keep full time employment. Myself and Jennie sat down and talked through our options, there didn't seem to be many, but nonetheless we tried our best to work through the situation.

Now, I have already mentioned that I was colour blind so a career in the armed forces or police was out of the question. The building trade was on its knees by this time and to make ends meet I was left with little option but to look elsewhere for employment. I now had a wife to care for, and it was my responsibility to do all I could to make sure this happened.

As I have said, I have always been one that likes a certain degree of formality and regulation in my job, and it was with a sense of trepidation that my parents asked us over one evening to their house to discuss something.

My mum being my mum, was looking through the Evening Standard for possible job opportunities she thought I might have liked, she happened upon an advert for prison officers, to say I was taken aback really does not do it 'justice', excuse the pun.

After all, you read some true horror stories about the prison regime, not only in this country but in others, and the thought of me entering a prison full of convicts, whilst not frightening, did give me a sense of unease.

However, I decided that it would not hurt to make an initial application, just so long as colour blindness was not an issue. I made some tentative enquiries to the prison authorities and asked them if my colour blindness would hinder any application I made to them? Their reply was simple in essence, colour blindness played no part in the recruitment stage, and would not hinder my career in the future.

With this in mind I carried on with the application and some six weeks later I finally heard back from the prison authorities, they were conducting interviews at Chelmsford prison within the next two weeks.

Myself and Jennie drove to the prison on the day of reckoning, with fingers crossed and hope in our hearts. This initial phase was an examination of logic and problem solving, followed by a multiple choice paper which would decide who would go through to the next stage of recruitment.

The exam lasted some two hours, and it was the longest two hours of my life. I thought it had gone pretty well, but you never know with these situations, for all I knew I could have blown my chance of having a steady career for any length of time.

What must be remembered is that even though I trained as a carpenter and joiner and my trade would have enabled me to get into Australia, I still had the mindset that maybe, just maybe it was possible to transfer to the Australian prison system once you had been excepted into the British prison system.

Anyway, it turned out that I had been successful in the

initial exam, and now they were conducting face to face interviews ten days later. I must admit that nothing prepared me for this interview. Once again it was at Chelmsford prison, but this time I had to go in front of a board of ladies and gentlemen and answer questions. It was terrifying, the walk alone to the table where the board members sat was at least a forty foot long, it was the longest forty foot I have travelled in my life.

I had prepared the best way I could, by speaking to other prison officers and finding out as much as I could from libraries and the media. The questions they asked whilst not being too difficult were designed to see the real you, and all in all, a logical head was needed at all times.

It took nearly five weeks for the authorities to let me know if I was successful. I was at this time still employed within the building industry and I remember receiving a phone call from Jennie saying that an envelope from the home office had arrived at our flat.

This was nine thirty in the morning and I still had another seven hours of work to do, so I asked Jennie to open it and let me know the result. This she refused to do as she said if I had been successful I should be the one who opened the letter.

I arrived home that evening around five forty five, had the normal cup of tea, two cigarettes, before I could even contemplate opening the envelope. Myself and Jennie sat on the sofa and decided this was it. With trembling hands and sweat dripping from my forehead I opened the brown envelope. I would like to say that I had no concerns whatsoever, but in reality I truly had no idea if I had been successful.

It transpired that I had been successful in my endeavours and I was given a phone number to ring where I would be told of the next stage in the recruitment process.

I commenced my training at Newbold Revel, Rugby. The course lasted nine weeks and would cover all the basics of training to become a prison officer. In truth, nothing can prepare you for walking on to the landing of a prison. All and sundry can tell you what to expect, but to walk into a real life prison full of inmates is not only an honour, but also one of the most frightening days of your life.

Application & Stress
****

Myself and Jennie had always talked about Australia as our future home, and we had no reason to think otherwise at this stage. We both knew that somehow, one day we would make Australia our home.

Even though I had started my new career within the prison service the initial pay was not all that high, and we had little savings from our previous employment. Whilst I enjoyed my time immensely within the prison service there was always a constant thought in the back of my mind that I had to return to Australia. Jennie was well aware of this, and she always backed me up on this matter.

After a year in the prison service it was decided between myself and Jennie that we should make every effort to get out to Australia while we still had the chance. As I said, I did enjoy my employment within the prison service, but as far as I was concerned nothing, absolutely nothing, would ever replace how I felt about Australia. It was always there, a need to return to a country that had a grip on me, this I still find hard to explain to the uninitiated.

I wish I could put it into words, but I cannot. It is as simple as that, it's just a feeling that no matter what I did or where I was, Australia and its people would always have a hold on me.

As many of you will know the migration process can seem very complicated, and at times extremely stressful. Things have not changed in this manner. The amount of paperwork that myself and Jennie had to compile and complete was at times totally confusing.

I should say at this point in time I am what you could call a 'perfectionist'. A lot of people blame this side of my character on the fact that I am a virgo, and I would hazard a guess that this has something to do with it. Many other people just call me an 'arse' for being such a perfectionist in most things I do, but it is a side of my character that I cannot change, no matter how hard I may try.

So you can imagine when myself and Jennie began the process of migration there were times I dare say she could have quite easily killed me. I must admit that this side of my character not only annoys the hell out of those around me, but also annoys me to my very core at times.

The times I tell myself to let things go, and try not to over analyse and investigate things in the minutest of details. So, if I annoy myself, God only knows what those around me think of me at certain times?

There are many good aspects of being a perfectionist, I believe that if a job is done it should be down to the best of my ability, and I also believe that all those around me should also do the best they possibly can. But certain aspects of being a perfectionist really do rub people up the wrong way.

The forms required, and the proof needed to back up any immigration application often seems impossible to collate and gather, and at times through absolute frustration the stresses involved can make you feel not only tired, but also ill.

However, after many weeks we had collated as much of the information that was possible. I must have checked the said paperwork at least one hundred times to make sure everything that was required was there. We sent the paperwork off recorded delivery, and thought however foolishly that would be the end of it, at least for a while.

After all, what else could be done? We had done all we could do ensure our application was complete in every way. There was absolutely no point in worrying any further. But this is the real world, the actual scenario was completely different.

To say that we were like a cats on a hot tin roof does not come anywhere near conveying the feelings that went through our minds. I know Jennie had the same feelings as well, to us it was a process that seemed to go on forever.

Each day that past was literally a living nightmare. There was not a second that went past that I did not have the application on my mind. My waking and sleeping moments were filled with thoughts of at times, extreme negativity, and at other times my thoughts were just off a positive outcome.

I couldn't concentrate on any one thing in particular, even though as I have said I had always done the best I possibly could in most avenues of my life it was still difficult to try and keep a sane and rational head on my shoulders, when my only thoughts were of the possibility of me and Jennie going to live in Australia.

As you would imagine, as I was a prison officer I had to have my wits about me at all times, and concentrate fully on the job in hand, to this day I don't know how I managed to do it, but somehow I did. That is not to say that each and every time I went to work my thoughts about Australia had lessened.

It goes without saying that not only did the migration process have a huge impact on myself and Jennie, it also had a huge impact on all those around me, not least those that I loved and cared about.

My parents did the very best they could to understand why we were thinking of emigrating to Australia, but past history, especially with my mum, did at times cloud her judgement. She never actually sat us down and said that we should not go, but it was obvious that she was not keen on the idea at all.

As I said, she never actually said we should not go, but reading between the lines you could see that she could not comprehend our decision. To her Australia was as alien as it had ever been. Even though she had lived out there for nearly a year, for her Australia brought back some very bad memories, and it was difficult for her to see our point of view.

No tempers were ever lost, or indeed was there any comment that was meant to be spiteful or hurtful, far from it. Though she did her best to back our decision, it was still difficult for her to accept that her son and daughter-in-law were going to a country that held few happy memories for her.

My dad has always been one not to make too much of a comment. He tends to keep his opinions to himself, unless it is an opinion that he thinks just has to be said. Again, whilst being very supportive and talking to us about the application process you could see that he was not at all happy. My dad really did enjoy Australia, and he could see our reasons for going, but once again, to have to say goodbye to your son and daughter-in-law must have been a huge wrench for him.

As with my mum, he never said a negative comment, but it was plain for all to see that he was going to miss us immensely if we were successful in our application. To tell you the truth I would not have had it any other way. If they had just shrugged their shoulders and said 'Good luck, get on with it', I would have been most upset. At least they were showing by their comments that they were going to be tremendously sad about seeing us go.

Many thoughts must have been going through their minds. Apart from the obvious ones like their son and daughter-in-law living on the other side of the world, they must have thought that at some point in time myself and Jennie would start a family.

Thoughts of grandchildren living in Australia many thousands of miles away from their grandparents would, I hazard a guess have been met with a sickening feeling, and made my mum and dad feel very sad at the prospect.

We had no plans for children at this stage, but we had always planned on having children during our time together, but from our point of view we didn't know when this was going to happen.

Looking back at that time it is only now that I have children myself that I can come anywhere near understanding how my parents felt about children, and indeed grandchildren. If either of my daughters told me that they were going to leave and live many miles from me I dare say I would feel sick to the very pit of my stomach.

Even if they only lived a couple of hundred miles away in this country I would still feel as if I had lost my right arm. So to try and comprehend how my parents felt when they heard the news that we were going to live in Australia is somewhat difficult, and the effect it must have had on them I am only just beginning to understand.

When you consider what I have just said, the thought of your children, let alone your grandchildren being many miles away must have had a huge impact. I worry constantly about my kids, and I would hazard a guess that no matter their age I will always do so, as any loving, caring and responsible parent would.

So God only knows what thoughts were running through my parents minds when we announced to the world that we were planning on living in Australia. OK, so by this time I was well into my twenties, but nonetheless this was never going to stop my parents from worrying. As they have always said, myself and my two brothers will always be their 'kids', and at times it is difficult to let us go.

Only now at forty six years of age do I really appreciate what they were saying, and to be faced with the same scenario as they were I truly have no idea how I would cope.

I have the advantage of having travelled extensively, and most importantly to Australia on many occasions, both on holiday and as a migrant. So I hope that if one of my children told me that they were going to live in a foreign land I would do all I could to understand. That's not to say that it would not be hard, but as long as they had valid reasons I will do all I can to understand their decision.

I dare say that there was not a day that went past that my mum and dad did not think of the future, and what that future meant now that their middle son and daughter-in-law were hopefully going to live in Australia. You can make all types of excuses and reasoning to backup your decision to emigrate. But at the end of the day the process of migration puts immense pressure not only on the applicants, but also on the people that surround them.

After all, the applicants are to some extent in 'control' of the situation, they have been the ones that have come to this decision, but the decision to emigrate was in some ways forced on those around the applicant's, and unfortunately no matter which way you look at it, migration will impact on their lives to a huge extent, there is no other way of putting it. To say that migration does not have an effect on the applicant's family and friends is to live in a fool's paradise.

I guess what I am trying to say here is simply this, that if you ever consider Australia as a viable choice for your future do not be under the illusion that it will not impact greatly on not only you, but all those around you.

Jennies family on the other hand were of a slightly different demeanour. If truth were known whilst I got on extremely well with the vast majority of Jennies family, I very rarely saw eye to eye with one particular member of Jennies family.

The reasons for this are still a mystery to me to this day. It is true, at times I could be difficult, we all are. I dare say there were sides of my character that she did not particularly like. But I loved Jennie with all my heart, and did all I could to make sure she was cared and loved in the manner that she so deserved.

At times the atmosphere between this family member, Jennie and myself was catastrophic. It was indeed an atmosphere of hate and absolute rage. Nothing I did or said was ever good enough. I could do no right in their eyes.

As you proceed to read further on into this book the reasons for their attitude may become somewhat clearer. But to try and understand them at times, was all that I could do.

They knew of our plans to emigrate and seemed to take the decision on their stride. My father-in-law who had travelled extensively for his job was of the opinion that we should make the most of our lives while we were still young, and he said as much to us on many occasions.

So it was with this atmosphere pervading that myself and Jennie carried on living our lives, or at the very least trying to live our lives with the constant worry of our formal application having been lodged with the appropriate authorities.

A New Beginning
****

Myself and Jennie thought of little else apart from our application. Each and everyday we would wake and the first words from our mouths would be something concerning Australia. We were getting in from work and yet again each and every word concerned Australia.

To say that we were living on a knife edge would be a massive understatement, there was not a second that went past that Australia wasn't on our minds. If truth were known, we had become migration 'bores'. In essence, people who talk, think and drone on incessantly about all things Australia. Our families whilst appreciating what it meant to us, must at some stage wanted to throttle our necks.

Day after day all we did was talk about Australia and the possibilities for our future. Any article or television program that had the barest mention of Australia would be viewed, read and dissected in the minutest of detail.

As the days went by it did take a toll on both of us, both physically and mentally. You find yourself in a place that is so unfamiliar that to try and cope with the situation takes all of your resilience, and to a certain extent makes you into a completely different person.

To have to wait for a decision that is completely out of your hands was a situation that neither of us relished, but knew was an integral part of the migration process. We had both done all we possibly could to ensure our application was as precise and correct as possible, but at times ideas of failure would inevitably creep into our psyche, and it was all we could do to keep our sanity.

After approximately six months, a timeframe that the immigration authorities had said was an average for a decision to be arrived at we were at our wits end. Our whole lives revolved around the morning post. Unfortunately I used to go to work at around six in the morning, so I normally missed the first post.

Bearing in mind that in those days mobile phones were in their infancy and my job necessitated that I was not allowed a mobile phone anyway then I hope you will come somewhere near appreciating the stresses and strains that were put upon myself, as I had no idea what had arrived in the post that morning.

When I was a prison officer we used to get a break in the morning at approximately 10:30 a.m, lunch was 12:30 p.m until 1 p.m, and then another break at around 3:15 p.m. On each and every break I would make my way down to the telephones that were located outside of the prison walls, and try and get hold of Jennie.

I would phone her at work, unfortunately her job often meant she was not available, and at other times it was impossible for her to take a phone call. So in essence, I was making these phone calls in a futile effort to try and find out the outcome of our application.

However, the day finally dawned that the envelope had arrived. It was on one of Jennies days off and she phoned the prison and left a message for me, unfortunately I was on escort duty that day and did not get the message until my shift was over.

I used to travel up to London on the train and underground system, and on a good day it used to take me around one and a half hours each way to get to and from work. That evening, I have never known time drag on as it did. I remember getting on the tube at Caledonian Road and all I could think of was where was the teleporter machine that would get me home in a couple of seconds?

Instead, I had to negotiate yet another packed tube, then change at Tottenham Hale to get the main line back to Essex. I didn't mind the journey most days, though it was long, I normally read a newspaper or chatted to a couple of other officers that went the some way as me, so this in essence this did make the journey less tiresome.

But on this day there was none of such niceties, the journey seemed to take forever, and to tell you the truth if someone had tried to strike up a conversation with me it would have fallen on stony ground. Not through any rudeness on my behalf, but purely because my mind was now fixated on getting home and opening the envelope that held our future.

After what seemed an eternity I disembarked the train and proceeded to walk to our flat. It was only a five minute journey, normally, but this was one short walk that might as well have been a marathon. My heart was beating ten to the dozen, my brow was oozing sweat, and my whole body was trembling. It is as clear today as it was then, I truly think that at this time in my life, even though a relatively young and fit man, I was very close to breaking point.

Keys were taken from my pocket, dropped several times, but eventually I managed to negotiate the lock and in I walked to our flat. I remember seeing Jennie sitting on the sofa hunched in a virtual fetal position, rocking backwards and forwards. I did not think that anyone could have been as nervous as me, but I think Jennie was very nearly at that point.

And there on the coffee table was a brown envelope, that in essence, held our future. A completely inanimate object that for all intents and purposes was going to either make us the happiest couple alive, or the unhappiest couple on God's green earth.

I had always been one to open the post as soon as I got in from work. It was a habit of mine that was an integral part of my being. However, on this occasion, and I don't know how I did it to this day, I managed to negate these feelings and proceeded to make myself a cup of tea and sit down.

By this time not a word had been spoken between myself and Jennie, I really don't think we knew what to say to each other. We were at a loss for words. We just looked at each other and we knew exactly what had to be said, nothing, absolutely nothing.

You would have thought that we would have been excited at the prospect of opening the envelope, but in reality the excitement was never there. Our feelings were of fear, trepidation, and absolute sickness.

I made another cup of tea for myself and Jennie and as was the norm, lit a cigarette. Still a word had not passed between us, not even 'Hello, how was your day'? A deafening silence had shrouded us in its blanket, and we truly had no idea what to say to each other.

It is clear today as it was back then, I remember lighting a second cigarette, looking at Jennie, and saying 'Well, shall we do it'? By this time we had both turned white, as the blood had drained away from our faces and it was all we could do to keep any semblance of sanity.

I changed seats and sat in the armchair, Jennie passed me the envelope, again without a word being said. I asked Jennie if she wanted to open it, but she refused, I don't think she was in any fit state to even do this simplest of tasks, the emotion she was feeling was that palpable.

My hands by this time were trembling beyond belief, and my insides were in turmoil, to say you have butterflies in your stomach is often an overused term, I did not have butterflies, I had a flock of seagulls.

Once again, I lit yet another cigarette, looked at Jennie, and said 'What are we going to do if we can't go'? The reply Jennie gave was simple in essence, and it was this, 'It will be fine, they have said yes'.

By this time I could barely bring myself to hold the envelope, and to open it seemed a near impossible task. However, I did eventually open it and for a few seconds, which seemed like hours, I tried to assimilate the information that sat in front of me.

The words written in front of me might as well have been written in ancient arabic, because my eyesight at this time was blurred because of the tears that were forming in my eyes. I am not normally one to cry, but the absolute stress and worry that I felt at this time had made me become an emotional wreck. My eyes were stinging, my stomach rolling, and the lump in my throat was as if I had swallowed a billiard ball.

It was as if someone had smeared vaseline across my

eyeballs, it really was that bad. A mist had appeared before my eyes, and all I could do to try and clear them was to blink ten to the dozen and rub them with my now sweaty, shaking hands.

After what seemed like hours I could just make out the first line. Jennie at this time was kneeling on the floor, head bowed, once again rocking back and forth in the fetal position. If she felt as I did then we were two of the most stressed out and worried people on God's green earth.

I read the first line at least a half a dozen times, and it was a sentence that had such an impact it is difficult to explain. I handed the letter to Jennie to make sure that what I had read was true.

We knew whatever response we got from the immigration authorities it would change our lives drastically. In reality, I have no idea how we would of reacted if we had received a negative response, thankfully that is a scenario that never took place. The first line of the letter simply said this, 'Dear Sir. We are pleased to inform you that your formal application to emigrate to Australia has been successful.'

We had received a positive outcome from the immigration authorities, and now we both knew that our lives were going to change radically, for better or worse, hopefully for the better.

We thought we had prepared ourselves for whatever the outcome. But in reality this was not the case. After all, none of us know how we are going to react until a certain scenario or situation happens to us on a very personal level. This was one of those times, we had never experienced anything on this scale before.

I had been with the prison service for just over a year, I enjoyed my work immensely, but there was always a cloud hanging over whatever I was going to do. That cloud was simply Australia. When I say cloud, maybe that is the wrong terminology, it was more a sense of Australia was calling me no matter the situation, and it was always going to be in my life.

I could have had the best job in the world, or rather, in my 'opinion' the best job in the world, and Australia would have still had this hold on me that would have made me return no matter what I was doing at the time.

To try and put this feeling into words is very nearly impossible, but we both had a sense, and a feeling of whatever was about to happen, whatever our future held, it was going to be the adventure of a lifetime.

We had tried to prepare ourselves for what had just happened. We had both in our imaginations tried to envisage what had just taken place. You would imagine the feelings of happiness and joy would have been completely out of control. But in reality it was really somewhat of an anticlimax.

After we had read that the immigration authorities had allowed us to emigrate all we felt was a deep sense of relief. There was no jumping up and down, no champagne corks flying through the air. No cheers and whoops of celebration. Just a feeling of absolute and utter relief. It was not until a few days after that the true impact of that day really hit us, a delayed reaction if you will.

The next step in our plans was going to be one of the most difficult times for us, and all those that we loved and cared about. We had to find a way of informing our loved ones that our plans had come together, and we were going to live in Australia. The both of us had often talked of how we should go about such a task, but in truth this never made it any easier.

The time had come where we were left with little choice but to try in some way lessen the impact of what we were about to do. We truly had no idea of how we should go about this. Perhaps we said to ourselves, we should just grab he bull by the horns and come out and say it.

All well in theory, but in practice a wholly different matter altogether. How do you tell your loved ones that you are about to emigrate, and am not sure when you will next see them?

We saw my parents on a very regular basis, and with this in mind I made a phone call to them to ask if we could pop over for a few hours for a chat. My parents are far from stupid, I have little doubt that they knew exactly what was about to be discussed, and I dare say they braced themselves for the conversation that was to follow.

To this day it has been one of the most difficult things I have ever had to say to anyone. To tell your loving parents that you are about to live on the other side of the world seemed to me, at that time, to be a kick in the teeth.

To me it was akin to saying thanks very much for the love and care you have given me over many years, but I am now going to buggar off to Australia. That is how I felt about it. Unjustified, too harsh, maybe, but the guilt I felt was immense. At the time it seemed as though I was the lowest of the lowest.

Of course my parents expected that if we got a positive response from the immigration authorities then we would in all probability go to Australia, but to be faced with the actual scenario must have been heart wrenching for them.

To say that migration only impacts on those that are actually involved in the actual application itself is to live in a fools paradise. It truly affects everyone who is merely a so-called 'bystander' during the event.

The evening we told them is burnt into my memory forever. The looks on their faces were looks of absolute, and abject sadness. There is no other way of saying it. My parents had always shown me love, support and tenderness. Of course we had our ups and downs, as any functioning family does, but they had always been parents that could not of done more for me.

They had always stood by me, helped me, and been people who I could always rely on for advice. They were, and are two of the most loved and respected people I have ever had the privilege to know.

To this day I thank God that they are my parents and not a day goes past that I do not think of them constantly. Now I was being a 'Judas'. I was telling them that I did not appreciate anything they had ever done for me, or at least that is the way I felt at the time.

Back 'Home'
****

Our plans to migrate were now in full swing, or rather we thought so. If truth were known we were wholly unprepared for what lay before us. Of course I had previously been to Australia, and 'thought' I knew everything about it, but when the reality started to hit home it was obvious that little, if anything was going to prepare us for what lay ahead.

Obviously myself and Jennie had made tentative plans as to where and when we would go to Australia. Perth being the most likely outcome as I knew the city very well, and had a few friends out there. When I say friends, I mean acquaintances. They had after all been my parents friends whilst we were in Australia, and to say I was close to them would be an exaggeration.

We booked our tickets for the eleventh of November and set in motion a series of events that would lead to us moving to the other side of the world.

Once again the scenario of goodbyes had to be done all over again. Only this time it was a different. When I left for Australia the first time I had just turned seventeen years old. I had no real responsibilities to speak of. My parents had taken all the necessary steps that were needed for our short-term move to Australia to take place.

They had the heavy burden and responsibility to make sure that myself and younger brother were cared for and looked after. This time it was my sole responsibility to make sure Jennie was OK and I did all I could to ensure this was the case. It was at times very difficult and agonising. Thoughts of how I would find employment once out there, where would we live in the long term, all manner of subjects that you could say had been on the periphery of our thoughts up to this point.

What was even worse was one simple fact. As a grown adult I was now faced with having to say goodbye to my parents and brothers. I had seen how my mother had reacted when we went to Australia previously, and that journey was only going to last a year.

This was a wholly different animal. We were now faced with migration. Not a big word when looked at in the grand scheme of things. An easy word to say, and to describe, but when looked at from a different perspective it is a word that is truly nightmarish when spoken of in terms of the emotional impact it has on all those involved, the applicants, and the innocent victims, our loved ones.

To say goodbye to my parents was the hardest thing I had ever done up to this point in my life. There have been times since when I have had to face other situations that were truly awful. But at this point in time this was the worst I had ever felt, about anything.

The looks on my parents faces were torturous and heart wrenching. I cannot ever remember seeing such pained expressions on anyones faces as I did that day. The looks are burnt into my very soul.

The day finally dawned that myself and Jennie were going to Australia. Even to this day to say goodbye to everybody on that morning still fills me with every conceivable emotion. Massive sadness, regret, excitement, trepidation, but above all, a sense that we were in some way being ever so treacherous in making the move to the other side of the world.

There was no way around this, the feelings of guilt and overwhelming sadness still fill me with emotions that I wish I could ignore. Now, bearing in mind this was over twenty years ago and the emotions are still as vivid now as they were then, I hope you can come someway near feeling the way we did at that time.

We boarded the plane on a cold November morning and did our very best to show those around us that we had made the right decision. However, I am sure we both felt this as much as I did. We really had no idea that this was the right decision, all we knew was that it was a decision we had thought long and hard about, and at the very least, a decision that was our responsibility.

The flight as always was long and tedious. But as you will recall I am one of the lucky few that can board an aircraft and within one hour fall asleep for the entire journey. Even at mealtimes if I am fast asleep the cabin crew would sometimes wake me to give me my meal, or sometimes they would ignore me and let me sleep.

Either way I can assure you that the twenty one hours it took to arrive in Australia was for me, a journey of little consequence, then as it is now. There are very few people that I know of that can sleep for the whole journey, and unfortunately Jennie is one of those people. She was never able to sleep for any amount time while she was in upright position, and whilst I do not have any real idea of how she felt, I can in some small measure sympathise, to a degree.

We arrived in Perth very early on a Tuesday morning. What must be remembered was that I had been here before. It was as if I was returning home once again. Jennie on the other hand had no experience of Australia at all.

For years I had banged on incessantly about how great Australia was, and in no uncertain terms told Jennie that she would love everything to do with Australia. What I had forgotten was simply this. The flight had been long as usual, and Jennie was shattered.

In my eagerness on arriving 'home' I thought Jennie would be as excited as I was. It is true that to some degree she was excited, and in her own way tried to share my excitement, but in reality all she wanted to do was sleep and recoup from her journey.

Even though Jennie did share some of my enthusiasm I could not understand her reticence to be as animated and excited as I was. I had after all, returned 'home'. Perth had changed little, maybe a little larger, but it was a city that once again captivated me, and once again seemed to welcome me with open arms.

That feeling that I had when I was seventeen came flooding back. My excitement knew no bounds. The inanimate object that was called 'Perth' once again enveloped me in its blanket of warmth, openness, and willingness to except and love me.

The same sounds and smells once again enraptured me in all their glory. Perth and its people were once again in my blood. The years of being away from a place I regarded as home had taken their toll on me. The emotions I felt were akin to seeing a long lost friend. All the effort and sacrifice I and others had made to make this possible had all been worthwhile, or so I thought.

We had arranged when we arrived in Perth to stay in a unit that had been organised by the of one of my parents old next door neighbours. Now bearing in mind, that I had done all the possible research into all manner of things regarding Australia you would have thought that our arrival would have been plain sailing, unfortunately, this was not the case.

We arrived at the unit, in a suburb of Perth that then, as it is now one of the more down market areas. Down market is a word I do not like using, but in the cold light of day it was a suburb that neither of us felt very comfortable in.

The lady in question had very kindly left a key out for us, and we entered the unit basically very tired and exhausted. What faced us was a living nightmare. One single bed, the smallest of kitchens imaginable, a toilet that was outside, and the unit as a whole was what could be described as a hut with the barest of amenities.

I had by this time as with most smokers worked my way through nearly twenty cigarettes after the long plane flight, and it was all I could do to yet again have several cups of coffee followed by several more cigarettes.

I told Jennie to lie down and have a rest whilst I decided to go out and look around our new home. As I said, the suburb in question was one of Perth's rather seedier areas, and to say I was shocked would be an understatement. Whilst I did not fear for our lives, I did fear for our sanity, and particularly Jennies. I made my mind up within half an hour that I would find a better suburb as soon as possible.

I went back to the unit after half an hour or so and just stared at Jennie lying on the bed, I began to wonder what I had done, but more importantly what I had done to Jennie and my family back in the UK. I was tired, emotional, and rather short tempered purely because we had both been on a long journey and arrived in a place that neither of us were going to be happy in.

At this moment in time I truly wished for a split second that we had never made the trip out here. It's amazing what effect tiredness and exhaustion can have upon you. Normally I would of seen the positive side to the situation we presently found ourselves in, I may of even found a funny side.

But this would of only been possible if I was thinking logically. At this exact moment it seemed to me as though I had the weight of the world upon my shoulders. I had pictures in my mind of my parents faces back in the UK. Tears running down their cheeks, filled with great sadness. I was well and truly wracked with guilt.

And then I would look over at Jennie. Her tiny body curled and hunched on a bed that was so unsuitable for a wife of mine. She looked shattered and exhausted beyond belief. All I wanted to do was to wake her and say sorry for what I had done to her. But I let her sleep some more while I decided our next move.

To say we had been let down by my parents friend would be a massive understatement indeed. I did have a phone number for her, but even though I was hopping mad I decided that at this juncture in time I would say nothing as this would only cause Jennie more upset, and that is the last thing I wanted to do.

When Jennie woke I told her not to unpack any bags, just take out the barest of essentials as we would be out of this 'hell hole' within a few days. It was a promise that I was determined to keep, and one that I did indeed keep.

The next few days were rather exhausting and stressful. I had all of the addresses of the real estate agents within Perth and I visited at least two dozen of them from my list of around fifty.

By this time exhaustion had really kicked in and my powers of observation and logical thinking were somewhat on the wane. If I had been thinking correctly I would of taken a lot more time to peruse our accommodation options, but such was the need for suitable housing I was somewhat hasty in my choice.

I eventually found a small bungalow in the suburb of Scarborough. This was no more than a half an hour's walk from the beach, had plenty of shops, and for all intents and purposes was ideal for what we wanted, or so I thought.

When we left for Australia we had very little money to speak of, after all, we were both relatively young and our savings would not last too long, in fact, I estimated that they would last no more than two or three months.

But one necessity of arriving in Perth was the need to purchase a car. We would need transport as soon as possible as this would allow us to find suitable employment.

I made the classic mistake of purchasing the first car I saw, it was an old Ford Escort that whilst having four wheels and a motor, wasn't what you would describe as 'luxurious', or indeed practical.

Our new house was on a relatively quiet street and fairly central to Scarborough that would allow travel in most directions. Whilst it was at least half an hour away from Perth city it was thought that by living in Scarborough it would allow us to live the 'Australian dream'.

Work was never going to be easy to find, but I was determined to work in any sphere just so long as it bought some money in. During the 1980's the immigration policy in force at that time allowed me to sign on with the local centre link office, where the government provided the minimum of money to live on, providing that I was an active job seeker.

As you will know by now I was a passionate fisherman and it just so happened that a small fishing tackle manufacturer was looking for someone to work in their warehouse. I was, even with all of the worries that I had, over the moon at getting such a job, and was looking forward to it immensely.

However, what I didn't realise was that by me going to work I would be leaving Jennie alone in the house for a substantial period of time. She had yet to find employment, and it was only now that I realised she was for all intents and purposes alone in a country that she knew little of, and to a certain extent, she had followed my dream of emigrating.

It was a dream I had for many years and now it had come to fruition. Unfortunately, I had taken Jennie along with me, I did at no time say to Jennie that she had to come, but I think deep down she knew that if we were going to have any kind of future she had to follow me to Australia.

Now these thoughts were planted in my mind and the responsibility I felt toward Jennie was immense. There was no getting away from the fact that Jennie had come out to Australia because it was my dream, and my dream alone to a certain extent.

No matter what was said, and no matter how happy she would be in the future she had still followed me to the other side of the world. These thoughts were now paramount in my mind, and as I said, to go to work and have these thoughts running through my head put an awful lot of pressure on me.

The house in Scarborough whilst being fairly comfortable, was quite old by Australian standards, and had obviously not been looked after particularly well. We had furnished it with the barest necessities, sofa, TV, bed, etc, but because of our money situation we could not afford any more.

As I said, it was fairly old by Australian standards and for this reason it had stood empty for a number of months. The real estate agent looking after the property took little interest in our complaints about the state of the house.

The water system was archaic, and at times we could not get any water to come out of the taps anywhere in the house. The décor also left a lot to be desired. Whilst I realised that this was only a small matter it still managed to get us both down. However, the main cause for concern, for Jennie especially was the wildlife that seemed to be sharing our abode.

Each and every morning I would wake and wait to see the next creepy crawly that had decided to infest our house during the night. I was used to seeing this fauna fairly regularly as I had lived in Perth before, and more to the point, South East asia. The nature in this part of the world can come as a surprise to the uninitiated, and at times it is fairly frightening.

So with this in mind I hope you can imagine the scenario in our house. Most mornings I would wake and the vast majority of the time I would be faced with at least two or three huntsman spiders doing all they could to scare the living daylights out of me.

Because of the type of furniture we had purchased i.e. pine, the huntsman's were somewhat camouflaged. I lost count of the times that I would sit in the living room to have a cup of tea and a cigarette, and within the space of five minutes I would see a huntsman spider move ever so slightly against the backdrop of the cane furniture.

Now I am not one to be scared of spiders, I have always had a massive interest in the natural world, but even the appearance, but more importantly, size of the spiders were indeed a shock to me. However, I would always put on a brave face and do my best to get rid of the spiders in the most humane way possible.

More often than not this would involve trapping the spider under a very large glass followed by placing a piece of paper underneath and putting the huntsman's back outside. Trouble is, no one tells you before you arrive in Australia how quick these spiders are. They would indeed give anyone a run for their money, and at times it was hilarious to see me trying to catch hold of one of the spiders whilst running around the living room in a pair of shorts, glass in hand, absolutely knackered.

Of course this all went on before Jennie got up, which I was thankful for. I used to get up at around 6:30 am and I saw it as my duty to do the spider 'patrol'. Fortunately the majority of the time I would succeed in my efforts and the house would be spider free by the time I set off for work.

We also had an old chimney breast in the living room, it obviously hadn't been used for many years, and also hadn't been sealed in anyway at all. We would often sit there at night and see a family of mice run up and down the now defunct chimney breast.

Whilst at first this aspect of our new house was rather shocking, it did give us a huge amount of entertainment, as many evenings were spent just watching the family of mice grow and make use of the living facilities.

It was something which we soon became accustomed to, and to tell the truth, was quite endearing. Endearing until one fateful day. I was at work as normal, just getting on with the normal day to day activities when my boss received a panicked and rather hysterical phone call from Jennie.

I tried my best to understand what she was saying, but the only words I heard were, 'Snake in the house'. The mere mention of the word snake had me running for my car keys, making my apologies to my workmates and boss and getting back to our house as soon as possible.

When I eventually got home I was confronted by Jennie standing in the middle of the garden refusing to any where near the 'bloody' house again. Once I had got her to calm down she explained to me that she had been in the kitchen when she heard a squeak from the living room.

Upon further investigation she said that all she could see was a snake sitting in the middle of the living room with what looked like a mouse hanging halfway out of the snakes mouth.

I tentatively went into the house not knowing what I was going to face. But there, in the middle of the living room was indeed a snake of around three feet long with just the barest of mice tail hanging from its mouth.

Now, bearing in mind that as I have said I learned as much as I could about Australia before we had arrived I took an educated guess at what type of snake it was. Whilst not being an expert, I did possess some skills in wildlife identification.

From what I could see this was a Tiger snake, I was not sure, but from the many examples I had seen in reptile parks etc, and the colouration, and the fact that we had a stream running at the back of our house my educated guess was that was indeed a tiger snake.

My main cause of concern was the fact that the snake had very nearly swallowed the mouse and would inevitably start to make its move fairly soon. As with most snakes, they will want to get away from human contact if at all possible. If I was to let this happen then there was no telling where the snake may end up.

So I took a decision that at the time I thought reasonable and well thought out. Looking back at this time maybe I should of done things differently, but the only thought that was running through my head at this time was the fact that Jennie really did not need this in her life at the moment.

So it was my responsibility to try and retrieve the situation in anyway I could. We had in the shed an old long handled hoe that looked as if it had been there since time began. I shouted for Jennie to go and get it, as I did not want to take my eyes of the snake in case I lost sight of it and it disappeared somewhere that we would never find him/her again.

Now many of you at this time will be saying that what I did next was both foolhardy and irresponsible, but what must be remembered is this. I had one thing on my mind and one thing only, the need to keep Jennie safe and make sure that she was OK, so with this in mind I hope you understand what I did next.

Jennie handed me the hoe through the living room window, and I then did my best not to panic or show her that there was any danger. The snake by this time had finished its meal and had its eyes squarely focused on me.

I had seen on numerous occasions how a professional snake catcher caught their quarry, I knew it wasn't easy, but at the time I had to do something. The handle of the hoe was around six foot long and I knew that if I kept this distance between me and our new found 'friend' then it would have little chance of actually striking me.

The snake was fairly lethargic at this stage so I made my move. I quickly made the move to trap the snakes neck against the floor with the end of the hoe. I was extremely careful not to put too much pressure on the snakes neck and I was successful in my attempt to trap the snake. The next stage of the exercise was somewhat more difficult.

I had to in some way negotiate my free hand and pick the snake up around its neck, ensuring that it could not bite me. To say I was nervous does not do the situation justice. I was scared out of my wits. But slowly and methodically I managed to inch my fingers up towards the snakes neck and grip it fairly firmly behind its head.

I then had to release the grip of the hoe and hope that my finger hold was good enough. This I did, and to my relief I had hold of the snake very securely. The snake by this time was doing all it could to disengage himself from my grip, and its whole body was tense and thrashing.

My next manoeuvre was one that I was dreading. How on earth did I let this snake go without it managing to bite me upon release? I was not going to release it anywhere near the house, so I walked at least half a mile down the road to a piece of scrubland that I thought the snake would appreciate.

The looks I received on my journey are burnt into my memory to this day. On two occasions a car pulled up and the gentlemen inside offered me a lift to the local reptile park. On the second such occasion I took up their kind offer as I thought it best if the snake was taken there, as if I released it where I thought appropriate it may find its way back to the house once again.

We arrived at the reptile park some twenty minutes later and made our way into the reception area. The Australian receptionist barely raised an eyebrow at what she saw. She just calmly picked up the telephone and within a minute or so a gentleman came through and extracted the snake from my grasp, the relief was palpable.

I explained to him what had happened, and though rather surprised he did give me a rather severe talking to about the stupidity of my actions. At this time I was not in a fit state to concentrate on anything, and his words fell upon stony ground.

My new mate, Simon, who had very kindly driven me to the reptile house insisted that he drive me back to our house and would here nothing of my objections. He had done enough in my opinion, but he would here little of it. The journey home became somewhat of an education in Australia humour.

At every opportunity Simon would insist that I was 'Stupid pommy bastard' for doing what I did. He was insistent that I was a fool and indeed, foolhardy, and if truth were known, I would have to agree with him.

We arrived home to see Jennie sitting on the lawn, white faced and completely devoid of any emotion except for several tears rolling down her cheeks. I and Simon did our best to comfort her, and eventually she did come around and we went back into the house.

After several cups of coffee and as many cigarettes I explained the situation to Simon and how it came about, we were both in agreement that the only reason the snake came into the house was because of the family of mice that we had living in the chimney breast.

That evening, though I am sure Simon had better things to do, we boarded up the fireplace and placed copious amounts of mice bait around the whole house. Simon to this day is a dear friend of mine and I cannot thank him enough for the kindness and generosity he showed myself and Jennie that day. We often talk about what went on that day, but he still insists that I was a stupid pommy bastard.

As I previously said, the money was fairly tight, but there came a point in time when we had little choice but to spend the money on an exterminator. This would involve the placing of powders and poisons around the house that would hopefully get rid of our lodgers who were living after all, rent free. I wouldn't normally have done this, but for Jennies sanity I thought it best.

My job at the fishing tackle warehouse was enjoyable, and to a certain extent fulfilling, but not once did I go to work with what could be called a clear conscience. I knew deep down that Jennie was left alone in the house for eight or nine hours, and it was all I could do to drag myself to work each and everyday.

Because of the accommodation, Jennies lack of being able to find work, and several other issues, the stresses and strains put upon us were getting more by the day. We didn't at this time have a phone connected in the house as this was going to put a strain on an already tight budget, so we would most weekends buy a phone card and phone the UK to talk to our parents.

We told them little of what life was like in Perth, I insisted that they did not know that our move had turned out to be one of regret and great stress. As far as they knew, everything was going fine, and all was well.

However, each and every time I spoke to my parents the emotion I felt was immense. I had always been very close to both my mum and my dad, and to hear them speaking to me so many thousands of miles away really did have an impact on me that was immense.

This impact would not have been such a problem if myself and Jennie had been far more settled in Perth. But in the cold light of day, our lives in Perth were hard, and we did not feel settled at all. Though my work colleagues were a genuine bunch of individuals they still could not take away the constant worry that I felt about our new lives, and in particular the concerns and worries I had regarding Jennie.

It didn't take long for us to look back at our time in the UK and think it wasn't so bad after all. Also the constant conversations to my parents each and every weekend I think contributed to our next decision, or rather my next decision.

We had been in Perth for no more than three months and it

was the longest and worst three months of my life. When I say this, I mean because of the way I felt about Jennie, even though she seemed very happy and put a brave face on, I felt as if the weight of the world was on my shoulders, and I had in someway let her down.

I had always told Jennie that Perth was a lovely city, which it was, and is, but in reality our lives just seemed full of worries, for the simple fact that I was going to work everyday and could not get over the thought of Jennie being left alone in the house for any length of time.

After three months it was more than I could bear, and I made the decision that we would both make our way back to England. There wasn't really any conversation or debate between myself and Jennie about this decision, I took it upon myself to make a decision that in the long-term, affected as both greatly.

We told our parents of our plans, and to say they were pleased would be an understatement. Whilst they talked us through our problems and worries, you could tell that deep down they felt an immense sense of relief and joy that we were going to return to England.

We had rented out our property in Essex and the tenants still had another five months of their contract left. Whilst the income from the rent just about covered the mortgage repayments, it did not leave any money left over.

So a decision was made that we would leave the property rented and fortunately we could move next door to my parents who had bought the property next door some years before for my mum's parents to live in.

Unfortunately they were now deceased so the property was empty. To say my parents worked hard to make our return as comfortable as possible would not do it justice. They brought new sofas, beds, and all the necessities that we would need in order for us to make it a home.

The Turning Tide
****

We arrived back in England rather jet lagged, and to all intents and purposes not knowing which way our life was going to go from here on in.

We were still very, very unsettled, for this I take full responsibility. After all, it was my decision to return to the UK, and I knew deep down that this had been one of the worst decisions I could of ever made.

I now had to live with the consequences of such a decision. I could see in Jennies eyes that she was not at all happy. But, a decision had been arrived at, and it was one that we were both going to have to live with.

My parents as ever did their very best to understand, and in some small way console us. After all, they had their son back in the UK and their daughter-in-law.

Bearing in mind that I wasn't exactly what you would call academic, the job situation was now of paramount importance. As I previously said, I had been employed by the prison service but had made the decision to emigrate, for better or worse.

I was, and am an extremely hard worker, and I would always do my best no matter what the scenario. So it was with this in mind that I started to look for work. I contemplated returning to the prison service, but there were several hurdles to overcome first.

Firstly, because I had chosen to leave the service any application I made would be looked at rather negatively. I cannot blame them for this. If I was in the same position I would have done the same.

Secondly, was the fact the prison service at this time was going through some rather radical changes in its recruitment policy. A lot of the services it offered were being put out to private tender, and staff numbers within the prison service were being cut, fairly drastically.

It was my responsibility to find work as quickly as

possible and make sure our transition back into the UK went as smoothly as possible.

There was always the possibility of going back once again into the building trade, but this too was having its fair share of problems. Job recruitment was at an all time low, and the jobs advertised were inundated with applicants. I needed to find work as quickly as possible.

I did a few odd jobs then was offered the chance to drive a taxi in and around my local town. I had always enjoyed driving immensely, and it was thought that this may be the best path to take.

The hours were long, but if you were prepared to do the hours then the money was there for the taking. I started driving a taxi in and around my local area. I did a mainly days, occasionally interspersed with a Friday or Saturday night. This not only topped up my earnings, but also I felt better about myself, as the decision to return to the UK had been mine and mine alone, and this had impacted greatly on my family.

Myself and Jennie went about our day to lives and we did our very best to make the most of the situation. Jennie had found employment back with what she knew best. She enjoyed the work immensely, and it was great to see her happy once again.

We were now in the position of where we could afford once again to buy a property in the UK. After many weeks we eventually found a suitable house and we moved in looking forward to our future. Even though we both seemed fairly settled in our new lives, there was very rarely a day that went past that we did not talk of Australia.

It was true that our first experience of Australia as a couple had been somewhat difficult. This was due mainly to my own stupidity and foolishness. If I had researched it properly and made a few adjustments before we left England I am sure that our transition would have been a lot easier.

But rarely did a day go by that myself and Jennie would not speak of Australia. We didn't want to settle in the UK. We both knew that our future lives lay elsewhere, and one day a return was inevitable.

Even though we were sure that our future lives lay in Australia we decided we wanted to start a family. Foolish some would say, but we did think long and hard about this.

I made some enquires to the Australian immigration authorities and in short they said that if we ever did want to return to Australia with a child this would not be a problem as we had a visa that allowed such a path to be taken.

To cut a long story short, in June of 1993 the arrival of our baby daughter Jane, bought us the happiness that should always be accompanied by the birth of a child. We were both over the moon, and the smiles on our faces were there for all to see.

It was around this time that I noticed a change in Jennie, she had started to become slightly depressed, I could not put my finger on when and why this change took place, but suffice to say it was noticeable to all those around her.

Being the person that I am I took full responsibility for this and thought it was as a consequence of us coming back to the UK. I wasn't sure if this was the reason, but in my own mind I was at fault, and there was no one else to blame.

I was doing all I could to ensure that Jennie and my young daughter were happy, and to a lesser extent, make sure that the whole of my family was happy.

At no point in time did I ever really think that we would make our long-term future is in this country, but at this present time it was a decision that I had made, and for better or worse I had to live with this decision, and make the best of our present circumstances. It was not easy, but nonetheless, I tried my very best.

I knew deep down, as did Jennie, that one day we would return to Australia. This time however we decided that we would do a lot more before our departure. However, there were one or two obstacles in our way to begin with.

The atmosphere between myself a certain member of

Jennies family was as ever, rather fraught and tense. I know for a fact that it had nothing to do with me taking Jennie to Australia, or indeed returning.

As I said, I have no idea why this situation came about. But it was obvious from the very beginning that they would never ever except me into their family. I did everything I could to facilitate bridges being built, and I did my very best to ensure that I never upset this particular family member.

To say there was pressure on myself and Jennie during our courtship and marriage from this particular family member would be an understatement. They would take every opportunity to castigate and deride me whenever they could.

Looking back at this time, and with hindsight, maybe I could of done more, I do not know how I would of gone about doing this, but I was always willing to do so to make sure that politeness was maintained, and a feeling of goodwill was somehow instilled.

But no matter what I did this family member would have never accepted me in a million years, I was for all intents and purposes flogging a dead horse. I will not go into too much graphic detail of exactly what went on between me and this family member, but suffice to say that at times I was driven to the point of distraction.

And if I was totally honest, there were times when I wanted to walk away from my marriage in a misguided thought that this would stop the ever more tense atmosphere pervading all of our lives. When I say 'wanted' could be misconstrued somewhat. I loved Jennie dearly and would of done anything, absolutely anything for her.

If this meant walking away from my marriage I would of done so. Because of the ever present bad will between this third party and myself, Jennie was often at times put in an awful position. I would often arrive home after a day at work and find Jennie in floods of tears because of what this person had said about me.

In my illogical mind I thought that the best thing to do at these times would be to give Jennie the option of separating from me. I thought that this would in some way stop the extreme stress and worry that she was under.

With this in mind, I hope you can understand that at times my life really was rather stressful and worrying. I had a young family that I was trying to look after, with constant thoughts of guilt for bringing Jennie back to the UK. I had my own family, mum, dad, brothers, who I knew deep down knew that we would return to Australia. These times were particularly hard for all those concerned, and at times I did not know which way to turn.

As time went by, myself and Jennie often discussed a return to Australia. By this time my daughter was approaching 18 months of age and she was indeed a joy, as she is now, most of the time!

The job I had taxi driving wasn't an ideal job, far from it, but it did keep the wolf from the door. I wasn't what you would call overjoyed at the thought of going to work every day driving a taxi, but as many millions of us do, we do these things in order for our family to live a relatively happy life.

Myself and Jennie as I have said, often spoke of a return to Australia, but at the present time this was thought not only impractical, but out of the question for one reason and one reason alone.

If we were to return to Australia we would be taking a grandchild away from its grandparents. To me a return to Australia would break the grandparents hearts. I wish that I was more selfish and self-centred, then this thought would have never crossed my mind, but I am not like that, and I hope I never become such a person.

However, after some heart wrenching conversations with my parents it was apparent that in order for myself and Jennie to be truly happy once again we would have to return to Australia.

No matter the heartbreak and sadness we would cause it was a decision that had to be arrived at, and all those involved would have to be told. It was not a situation myself or Jennie relished, but a decision nonetheless that had to be made for our long-term happiness.

We had previously discussed whereabouts in Australia we would try and resettle. Jennie never really liked Perth, when I say that I really mean she never really felt at home in Perth. To her even though it was Australia, it was still just another big city, but this time, with much more sunshine.

As I said at the beginning of this book I had always been an obsessive fishermen, and when you speak of fishing in relation to Australia there is one place out there that stands head and shoulders above all others, and that is Cairns.

Cairns was, and is, the marlin fishing capital of the world, and it had always been a dream of mine to visit and possibly live there. With this in mind we decided that this would be our next home in Australia. Totally impractical maybe, but at least a decision had been arrived at.

This time we were going to try and do it differently. It was decided that I would arrive in Cairns at least two weeks before Jennie and my baby. This we thought would give me time to sort out accommodation and find work.

Once again on the fateful day the goodbyes to loved ones were as heartbreaking as ever. No matter how many times I have been to Australia I still find it tremendously difficult to say goodbye. No matter if I am only going for several days on business, or for an extended period of time. The hollow feeling I get in the pit of my stomach is always there.

Cairns. A Dream Shattered
****

I flew out to Cairns and arrived on a very warm and humid February morning. I would like to say that Cairns was what I had expected. But nothing could be further from the truth, it exceeded all my expectations, and then some.

The sights, sounds, and more importantly, the unique 'feel' of the place was to this day, awe inspiring. It was everything I had expected it to be, and more. Whilst I could of very easily let my mind become distracted I knew I had to source accommodation, and find a job as soon as possible in order for Jennie and my young daughter to come out.

Within a matter of two days I had already found somewhere for us to rent. It was a lovely open plan bungalow, three bedrooms, large kitchen, and massive living room. This time with approximately a quarter acre of land. The house was in the suburb of Edmonton, a relatively new building project with one overriding advantage.

It was set amongst the backdrop of the tropical rainforest. Indeed, the front door of our new property was only a ten minute walk from the rainforest.

The property was unfurnished as was the norm back then, so it was down to my interior designing skills, of which I have very little, to try and source materials to make the house look nice for when my family came over.

I bought a wicker sofa, two armchairs and two beanbags. From the second hand store I bought a TV, and video recorder. The bedding was purchased from the sale a local store was having, and within three days I thought I had the property looking as Jennie would want it to be.

I was at this point in time exhausted, and for all intents and purposes I could have quite easily just laid down and slept for a week. All the time I had to in my own mind, make sure that this time things were going to work out, and we could all put roots down in Australia, and make it our new home.

This time I was going to do things very differently. I had already found a house that was relatively new. Spotless in décor, and set in a suburb of Cairns that was extremely nice and welcoming. Hopefully this time I had done things correctly.

Jennie and my baby arrived some two weeks later, and I'm glad to say was very impressed with what I had done to the house. I had been on tender hooks for some time not knowing how Jennie would react to my interior design skills, but thankfully all was well, and the weight that was lifted from my shoulders was palpable.

Bearing in mind, that this was February in Cairns the heat and humidity were at times stifling. We had experienced heat in Perth before, but nothing compared to this. I had heard stories about the heat and humidity in North Queensland, but until you have actually experienced it the conditions are very difficult to try and explain.

My next concern was the need to find gainful employment. I knew before I arrived in Cairns that this was not going to be an easy thing to do, but I have always been an optimist and when push comes to shove I will do all that I can in order for all around me to be happy.

I went to the local centre link office and enrolled in their job employment scheme. As expected this was not going to be easy. And after weeks of looking for gainful employment I was becoming somewhat disheartened.

However, we had by this time become very good friends with our next door neighbours. A young couple with no children and who had their own business. Steve, the young man in question was an extremely hard working baker and he was in the middle of setting up his own business. His mother, who was a lady in her late forties heard of our plight and offered me some part-time work within her company.

Her business was to erect promotional banners and posters in and around Cairns of upcoming events that businesses and stores were participating in. This would often involve working late into the night as a lot of these banners and posters had to be erected when the shopping malls were closed and clear of customers.

I enjoyed my work immensely, always having a laugh and a joke with the fellas around me, but the work was still only part time and was just enough to keep myself and young family going.

Jennie was always what you would call very maternal and loved children. Our daughter, loved and cared for by both of us, was a joy to behold. If truth were known at this time I was becoming somewhat concerned that I seemed to be having less contact with my daughter. I excused this as just a fact of working some silly hours, and the opportunities to spend time with Jane were becoming rare.

When in reality it was Jennie who seemed to be making the situation worse. Each and every time I went to play with our daughter, Jennie would often step in and take over the situation. I excused this behaviour and just thought that it was me being paranoid to some degree. Jennie after all had the patience of a saint, and nothing was too much of an effort for Jane.

But I dismissed the thoughts that I was having about Jennie as inconsequential and silly. After all, we were all very tired and my imagination must have been working overtime, or so I thought.

We had always known that we wanted more than one child and it was only a matter of time before this came about. Myself and Jennie had planned for several months on having another child and it was decided that even know our resources were fairly well spread we would try for another baby.

Within five weeks of us trying Jennie confirmed to me that she was indeed pregnant, whilst I was not shocked, I was somewhat surprised at how quickly this had come about. I have never been one to show my emotions to anyone, and this was to be no different.

I was indeed over the moon and full of the joys of spring, but it is a side of my character that I very rarely show this to anybody. All I knew was, that a new baby was on the way and to me, my life was now complete.

We did the normal registering at the local hospital, doctors surgery, and prenatal classes and got ourselves ready for the arrival of a new baby.

Jennie had never been one to moan, but at times I could see that the weather conditions were getting her down somewhat. The heat and claustrophobic humidity took its toll on me, so god knows how hard it was for her?

By this time I was working full-time for my neighbours mother and I was beginning to enjoy the work, and the rather strange hours. My wage packet went up considerably, and it seemed at last as if everything was finally coming together for us as a family.

Jane, our youngest daughter by this time was just over two years old and she seemed to be loving every minute of Australia, we did our best to explain to her that she would soon have a new brother or sister, and I think in her own way she took this in, and was eagerly expecting the arrival in the very near future.

On the 5th August 1995 myself and Jennie with little Jane in the pushchair decided to take a walk down to the pier marketplace. This shopping precinct whilst not being the biggest in Cairns, did overlook the harbour and mud flats. It was always a pleasant walk, and we would spend hours trying to see the crabs that were busy making their home in the newly washed sand. Jane was fascinated by the wildlife on show.

However, this day was different. A replica of 'HMS Discovery' was moored at the marketplace. Whilst I have never been one for naval history I did relish the thought of having a look around this replica and trying to find out as much as I could.

Myself, Jennie, and Jane had just disembarked the replica when Jennie looked at me and said 'I think the baby is on its way'. Obviously, I had been through this before, but my experiences with Jane really did not hold me in goodstead for what was about to take place.

The hospital was no more than a fifteen minute walk from where we were, but as you would have gathered Jennie was in no condition to walk, so in one mad rush I went to the car park, got the car and drove our family to Cairns Base Hospital. The time was approximately 2:10 p.m.

I had expected at least a couple of hours to get myself ready for the forthcoming event. However, within 10 minutes of arriving at the hospital the midwife on duty told myself and Jennie that the baby was going to be born, very, very soon.

Now, when I say very, very soon, I thought this would give us at least some breathing space to collect our thoughts, but at 2:50 p.m. our new baby was born. Labour had been no more than thirty minutes and it was indeed a shock to all of us.

We had always known that the new baby was a girl, but to see our new daughter as a newborn was indeed a miracle to behold. I have never been one to go gaga over babies, I still think they are a miracle, but to say that I adore babies would be stretching a point, even my own babies, sorry kids.

Please don't get me wrong, I love children dearly, but babies to me just seem to be either crying, screaming or doing the unthinkable in their nappies, and it is not until they are about eighteen months old that I seem to have any connection with them. I know, that sounds harsh, but in reality that's just the way it is.

Obviously, the phone calls were made to family and friends back in the UK and they were over the moon with what had happened. As is the case in most loving families the news of a grandchild is met with great joy and happiness.

I cannot come anywhere near putting myself in their position of knowing that a grandchild had been born on the other side of the world, and not being able to hold or even see them. It is only now as a parent myself that I can truly imagine in the minutest of detail the feelings that both sets of parents must have felt.

We were both still relatively young and in as much did not

have the wise heads we have now. As many of you will know, the birth of a child truly does change your life drastically, may I add, for the better. I know at times it may not seem for the better, but I can assure you it is.

It was at this point in time that I noticed the small but obvious change in Jennie become a little more evident. At that time I could not put my finger on it, but she did change to some degree. Firstly, I put this down to the arrival of a new baby, sleepless nights, worrying about their health, and all in all, just general tiredness.

But as time went by I could see the change in Jennie gathering momentum, and it was a worrying facet of our new life down under. Looking back at this time, I guess I would not have done anything differently, all I tried to do was keep my head down, plug away, and do the best I possibly could for my family.

I am in a position now of being able to look back at this time with hindsight and I should of seen the warning signs. But as you will discover later on in the book if truth were known, I truly had no idea what was about to unfold, and how I should have dealt with it.

It is true that for all intents and purposes we were extremely happy, we had Jane and now our youngest addition 'Betty'. My life was complete in every way. A loving wife, two happy and healthy children, and living in a country that I had dreamt about for many years.

Each and every weekend we would take ourselves down to the beach, or to the rainforest and we would enjoy our time immensely. There was no evidence of the traumatic, and at times life threatening scenario that was about to be played out around us.

We had very good neighbours on both sides of our house, which helped immensely. They not only helped us assimilate into Australia a lot quicker, but were also becoming very dear friends. Anything we asked of them was never too much trouble and they always said that whatever they could do, they would do all that they could.

By this time, Jennies whole persona was changing somewhat, it was as if she was becoming a different person. I did my best to try and cope with the situation that was unfolding before my eyes, but at times my frustration and worry got the better of me, and it was all I could do to shout at Jennie and ask her what was the matter?

Yes, she was tired, we both were, after all, a new baby is bound to do this. She had made some really good friends in Cairns through a local playgroup, and they were great source of support and inspiration to her, but I was feeling gradually more and more alienated by Jennie and her attitude.

There were times when I was completely ignored, and on many an occasion I was not allowed near the children. I know a lot of people will put this down to my imagination, and say it was jealousy on my behalf, but nothing could be further from the truth.

All I wanted to be was part of the family, and to be included in all its activities. But at times I was completely excluded, and felt as if I did not belong, at all. I did my best to overcome this, and put it down to the strain of a new baby and new country. But at times I admit I did lose my temper through sheer frustration and worry. This would result in me asking Jennie in no uncertain terms what I had done wrong? I could not understand why I was being more and more pushed to one side.

Jennie would not, or as I found out a lot later, could not, explain to me what was going on. Whilst she knew she was acting in a very strange way there was nothing she could do to change her behaviour.

At that time I wanted to blame her, and say to her why is she treating me like this, and on occasion I did, but I was met with the normal response from Jennie, 'I don't know why I feel like this, it's just the way I am'.

I did my best to try and assimilate what Jennie told me, but nonetheless it was still very, very difficult for me to accept. I am not quite sure when it happened, but I did blame myself for the way Jennie was acting. I blamed myself for everything that was going wrong.

I began to think that maybe she was missing her family, and she felt guilty about taking two grandchildren to the other side of the world. Everything I did, everything I said was wrong, there was no right that I could do.

I took it upon myself that I would try and rectify the situation and cope with what was going on with a level head. But these are just words, and words are very empty when they cannot be backed up by actions. Every action I took to ensure our happiness seemed to have little impact, and Jennies whole persona was one of negativity, and at times hatred towards me.

Nothing I did seemed to work. I remember one occasion when I had the opportunity after getting in from work to cradle my youngest daughter. I slumped back into the beanbag that was in our bedroom and just sat there and looked at the little bundle that was falling asleep in my arms. It had been no more than ten minutes when Jennie walked in and without hesitation said to me, 'Give me my daughter, she has to be with me'.

I was at a loss as to what to say. What had I done wrong? All I had ever tried to do was look after my family the best I possibly could. I admit, that I had made many mistakes along the way, as we all do at times.

But I had done little to deserve this sort of castigation. I had never used physical against Jennie, nor would I ever dream of doing such a thing. I occasionally lost my temper and said things that I later regretted, again, as we all do. But in all honesty I had always tried my very best when it came to my family, I could do no more.

Of course I knew that at certain times women after having a child can suffer to some degree with depression. Sometimes this can be minor in its appearance, but it can be catastrophic. But this was different. Jennies behaviour had changed ever so slightly while we were still back in the UK after the birth of Jane, and now there seemed to be no way of helping her.

I had noticed a minute change in her behaviour before we departed for Australia and now, this second time. But now her behaviour was becoming even more irrational and out of control. There seemed to be little I could do about this.

However, I did come to one conclusion. I convinced myself that Jennie was unhappy in Australia, and it was all my fault. No matter the excuses I made, or indeed the reasons I came up with, however valid I put forward for her behaviour, there was only one conclusion that I could come to.

It was simply this. That I was the one person that was responsible for the way Jennie was acting. I did however blame one other thing for the way she was behaving. I blamed Australia in no small measure.

Illogical and irrational I know, but this is with hindsight. At that particular time I blamed myself and Australia. No matter what Australia had meant to me in the past, it was now viewed by myself as a country that was taking the woman and children that I loved so much away from me. I began to despise everything about the country and the people.

Once Australia had meant everything to me, once it had been a part of my life that was an integral to me as my right arm. But now it was a place that I resented in every conceivable way. How dare it take away from me the family that I loved to the ends of the earth?

It was for these reasons that I said we would travel back to the UK where I thought the love and support of both Jennies and my family would make her feel better. In my ignorance, I believed that she needed both sets of families around her to make her feel more comfortable and confident, and maybe then she would become the woman I first knew.

I remember telling Jennie of my intentions to go back to the UK and take our young family with us, I don't know what reaction I expected, all I knew was that I had to do the best I could, and this was the best I could possibly do.

Jennie said time and time again that she did not want to go back to the UK, and at times pleaded with me for us to stay in Australia. These were the times when she would talk to me with some degree of civility, but I could not understand why the rest of the time she was so unforgiving of all I did and said.

No matter the pleas from Jennie, and the arguments put forward, my mindset was now one of negativity, and the only thought I had in my mind each and every waking moment was a return to the UK where Jennie could be better looked after.

After all, no matter what I did and said she never seemed to respond to anything that I did. I even suggested that we go to the doctors and explain what was going on. In my naivety I thought Jennie may be suffering some kind of breakdown. I did not know the reasons for this, except that it was all my fault for dragging her to a country that I now hated with every sinew of my being.

Once again my mind was made up. By this time I had become accustomed to making the phone calls back to the UK concerning our plans.

The day arrived when we were due to fly back to the UK, I remember the removal company had stripped just about all of our belongings from our house, and there was just me, Jennie, Jane and Betty sitting on the living room carpet staring into emptiness.

Even at this stage Jennie asked me to reconsider my decision, and she assured me that she would be far happier in Australia. But no amount of pleading was going to change my mind. All I knew was that if I could get Jennie back to the UK, surrounded by familiar things she may become the person I once knew.

Meltdown
****

We arrived back in the UK extremely downhearted and sad. I remember looking at Jennie as the 747 touched down at Heathrow airport and there were tears in her eyes, I cannot remember exactly what my thought process was at this time, but I knew in my own mind that I had made the correct decision, or at least I hoped so.

We were welcomed in the terminal by my father and it was as if we had never been away. Of course he was extremely happy to have his son back in the bosom of the family fold, but deep down I think he knew that we were not truly happy with the decision we had arrived.

As with most things in life you can only live with the decision you have made at any one particular time, and my decision had been to come back to the UK, to try and make Jennie happy once again. I was not to know the story that was about to unfold would change not only mine, but everyone else's life, radically.

Once again we stayed with my parents and a long and drawn out process of trying to find work and accommodation was again played out. You would have thought that we had all got used to this by now, but in reality it is still a situation that most of us find rather stressful, and at times, very tiresome.

Jennies demeanour at this time was getting no better. I was for all intents and purposes beginning to feel as if I was not wanted any more. Please don't misread what I have just said, Jennie would never at this time actually say to me that I was not wanted, but nonetheless it was a feeling that was overwhelming to me.

I was not at any stage allowed near my children, maybe for the briefest of moments I would be allowed to pick them up and play with them, but only when this was played out in front of family and friends. Once we got back into our own world I was once again pushed to one side and made to feel completely inadequate.

We eventually found a house in the depths of Hertfordshire, it was mid-terrace and was indeed a lovely family home. Set amongst some very picturesque and stunning scenery. But, the situation between myself and Jennie really was getting no better, and the added pressure of a third party just made me feel even more inadequate.

I was at times made to feel totally useless. I admit, that at times I can be one of the most frustrating people to live with because of an attitude of perfectionism and wanting to do the best I can for those that I love. Unfortunately, that can come across as being somewhat controlling. 'Controlling' is a word that encompasses a lot of emotion.

And I guess, if I were completely honest with myself I have to realise that this side of my character can at times drive people away. All I ever wanted, and want, is to help those around me, but unfortunately as I have said, this can come over in some people's eyes as very controlling.

I found employment at a local building company where I was employed as a carpenter and joiner. The job bought enough money in to support my family and enabled us to have some kind of life.

What must be remembered through all of these trials and tribulations is that Australia still played a huge part in not only my life, but all those around me. You would have gathered, and will gather that Australia means a lot to me, but I would of sacrificed any feelings I had for Australia to make my home life far more happier.

The deterioration of my family life, and any future family life that I had continued. I could still not put my finger on why things were going so wrong between myself and Jennie. All I knew was that Jennie seemed to be getting further and further away from me, and nothing I did, said, or tried had any impact at all.

As I said, the influence of a certain family member never

helped the situation at all. They were never going to except me, and would do all they could to make my life hell with their comments and actions. In Jennies defence she never really took any notice of what was said about me by this particular person, but deep down it must have had some impact.

All I knew was that my home life was now non-existent, and I had tried my very best to try and talk to Jennie about how I felt and what was going on, but each and every time was met with negativity and an overwhelming feeling of sadness surrounded me.

I was losing the two things in my life that made me what I was, a husband and dad. Without these two things I could see little point in living. I had no idea of which way to turn next. The love I felt was as strong as it had ever been, unfortunately the love Jennie felt for me had disappeared, or so I thought.

A Life Torn Apart
****

The day finally dawned when Jennie asked me to leave the family home, it was a scenario that I knew would have to come, but one that I had refused to acknowledge up to this point.

At this point in time my parents as ever were supportive and loving. Not once did they apportion blame to any one individual. I told them in very broad terms, what had been going on, and my reaction to it, in other words to say how I 'felt'.

Even at this point in time they did not pass comment, they just let me know that they would be there for me if I needed them. And god, did I need them now. They were as always, there for me, and to this day I cannot thank them enough.

All I knew was that my family was now gone and I could not see a way of getting them back. If any of you have ever gone through a separation and divorce you will know it is one of the most agonisingly stressful times of your life, and one that I would not wish upon my worst enemy.

Being as I am, I had told Jennie that in order for her to be happy I was quite prepared to walk away from our marriage in order for her to carry on her life, and hopefully she would find happiness with somebody else down the line. I truly meant it, I would have done anything to make Jennie happy, and if this meant me not being part of her life in the future then this was a sacrifice that I was well prepared to make.

I did however ask that I could still see my kids on a regular basis, and if at all possible still have an influence in their young lives. At this point in time I realised that things were not going to be as easy as that. The third party involved who had always taken a huge dislike to me made it quite obvious that they would do all they could to keep me apart from my children.

As I previously said, I was not perfect by any stretch of the imagination, but I had always done my best when it came to my family. However, there was one overriding reason why this relative would from now, make my life a living hell.

I will admit that I am one of the few parents out there who believe that a quick tap on the back of the legs if children are misbehaving badly does not hurt. I am not speaking of 'violence' against children, hitting children, or using undue force against children. But I do to this day believe that a tap on the backside, or the wrist in the very rare circumstance does no long-term harm.

I know that we all in this so called 'enlightened' age seem to have an opinion on how best to discipline our children, and at times the debates can become somewhat heated. But my school of thought whilst being rather 'old fashioned' in some peoples views, is one that I feel right for me.

With this in mind I would like to highlight the one particular issue that was to impact on my life greatly. When myself and Jennie were still together Jane was being extremely rude and belligerent toward Jennie one Sunday afternoon. I asked Jane on numerous occasions to stop it and calm down. But this was to no avail, she just kept being very rude and belligerent. To this day I cannot remember exactly what she was doing, as I think I have tried to erase the memory from my mind.

Anyway, Jane carried on, and I decided to step in before the situation escalated, she turned and said something to me, which made me say to her 'Get up those stairs now, and calm down in your bedroom'.

As she ran up the stairs she was still being rather rude and shouting back at me. I decided that I had quite enough of this and I followed her upstairs. As I followed her up she ran into her room screaming and kicking as she went as was the way with her at this time, she was, and is still at times, very forceful in her opinion, and this was one of those occasions.

As she ran into her bedroom she tripped on the carpet rail between her room and the hallway, as she tripped she did not get her hands down in time and her face hit the floor. Even though her room was carpeted the force of the impact was quite hard.

As I picked her up I could see that there was blood coming from the mouth, and she had knocked one of her front teeth out, or rather, it was hanging by a thread of gum. Even though there was not a lot of blood, it was still shocking to see my young daughter with a tooth hanging down from her mouth, and blood seeping from her lips.

I cradled her in my arms and went downstairs and said to Jennie we would need to get her to hospital as soon as possible as the tooth was broken but had not quite come out. Jennie looked at me, and I'm still not sure to this day if she believed me. I explained to her what had happened, but because of her mindset at this time I do not know what she was thinking.

She had always been witness to myself disciplining the children, and though she may not of particularly liked it, she could always see why the children on very, very, rare occasions got a tap on the backside. Jennie herself never told the children off in this manner. She would always talk to them first in the hope that this would placate them. Normally it did so, but on occasion I would have to take the bull by the horns and step in.

It was never a scenario that I enjoyed or relished. On the very rare occasion that I would step in and give my children a tap I would be filled with guilt and an overriding sense of failure, but it was a situation that had to be faced, no matter how distasteful at times.

When we arrived at the hospital the doctors as normal took great care of Jane, they extracted the whole tooth, and gave her three stitches in her top gum. The doctors said that hopefully the new tooth would come through in time, and there would be no long-term effects of the accident.

However, judging by the looks on the doctors and nurses faces I could see that some of them did not believe me. For this I cannot blame them. They must see on many an occasion children brought into accident and emergency who have indeed had 'violence' used against them, and I guess at least we should all be grateful that any child taken to hospital with such an injury is looked upon with some degree of skepticism.

This episode in my life was one that was going to haunt

me for many years to come. As I said, the third party involved was a person of an extremely vindictive and cruel personality. I was due to find this out in no uncertain terms within the next few weeks and months.

The Law Is An Ass
****

Because of the separation between myself and Jennie I was by this time virtually bereft of emotion. I was not only emotionally drained, but also mentally I was not what you would call in a 'stable' condition. My whole world had fallen down around my ears, and it was all I could do to get up each morning and face yet another day.

Because I had moved out of the marital home I yet again stayed with my parents, who just like on many previous occasions had shown me so much support, care and love. It was at this point in time that I started to receive solicitor's letters addressed from Jennie.

The vast majority of these letters I could cope with, they were normal, if 'normal' truly conveys what I'm trying to say, but they were letters that dealt with the specifics of a formal separation. Money, housing, and all of the other peripherals that are integral to any formal separation between husband and wife.

But one day I received a letter outlining the access I would have to my two children. It basically said that I would be allowed to visit my two children as and when it was deemed fit by their solicitor involved.

Whilst I didn't care less about anything else that had gone on, within reason, I wanted to be assured that I would be able to see my two girls. I wasn't sure which way to turn, for many reasons, the least of which I had never gone through this before, and if truth were known, I was in no fit state to fight any of the legalities that were involved.

I took advice from those close to me, and they advised that I should seek the professional opinion of a solicitor as soon as possible to try and sort out the access to my children.

I remember the day as if it was yesterday, a day like no other, and one that will remain with me until my dying day. I had made an appointment with a local solicitor who was known to the family. I waited in the reception area not really knowing what I was going to say or do, all I knew was that I was going to insist that I could see my children again.

Nigel, the solicitor in question, asked me into his office and he started to explain the situation that was unfolding. Without going into too much detail about the more mundane aspects of divorce, he did make one point very, very clear. It was simply this, that I was to be denied access to my children for the foreseeable future.

As you would imagine I was truly shocked and gobsmacked at what had been said to me. I cannot remember what I said next, but I dare say it was trying to find out the reasons why.

Nigel explained to me that it had been bought to his attention through the other parties solicitors that I had punched Jane in the face, and not only knocked her tooth out, but also knocked Jane out, this then required medical attention. There are no words to describe how I felt at this point in time, if I thought my life was wrecked before I went to see Nigel, it most definitely was now.

The so called evidence for this was the situation myself and Jane had found ourselves in when she ran into her bedroom on that fateful day. But even more surprising was other 'evidence' that had come to light.

As with most children of Janes age they want to do certain things in their lives that make them happy and fulfilled. For this reason Jane some months previously had been taking dance lessens. Every Saturday morning myself or Jennie would take her along to the dance class and wait the hour or so until she had finished.

The last several months however of these dance lessons I was not allowed to take Jane as the situation at home was becoming even more frustrating.

I would sit at home awaiting their return. When they arrived I would as any loving parent does ask how the lessens went and ask Jane if she had enjoyed herself? Jane would normally be in full flow with how excited she was, but inevitably Jennie would hurry her away for any number of reasons.

Nigel then proceeded to tell me that Jane, whilst at these dance classes had been questioned by the teacher about several bruises that were on her legs, particularly the shin area. I asked him to expand on this, as I was at this point in time, truly confused.

Nigel said that the reason Jane had stopped going to dance lessens was that Jennie could no longer cover up the brutality that I was using against Jane. She had 'allegedly' been in an awkward position and refused to take Jane to the lessons as the embarrassment of these bruises was too much.

I explained to Nigel that as far as I was concerned Jane stopped going because she had become bored with the lessons. Jennie had told me that Jane no longer wanted to go as she was indeed bored. At that time this did not surprise me in the least. As with most children of Janes age their concentration spans can at times be minimal, and it is only a matter of time before they become fixated on their next adventure. At no point in time had anyone said to me that it was for any other reason. Now I was once again being accused of the most violent acts known to man.

The truth was simply that Jane, being the age she was often played, ran, fell over, bashed into objects, etc, and the bruises on her legs were a natural outcome of her being a kid. Not once was there a bruise that I would be overly concerned about. They were just a natural occurrence of 'growing up'.

I was, and have always been a person who looks upon each individual with fairness, and I like to think that there is some degree of humanity in all of us. However, I was sorely mistaken when it concerned certain members of Jennies family. I could not believe that someone could be as cruel and as vindictive as this. They basically had the ability to stop me seeing my two children for the foreseeable future.

I walked out of Nigel's office a broken man, I had no idea what to do next in order that I could see my children again.

Suffice to say that I went back to my parents house and I'm not ashamed to say this, was hysterical beyond belief. I am not normally one for tears, but I truly did lose the plot that day, and my life could have ended there and then, and I would not have cared less.

Several days and weeks went past, and Nigel informed me of every letter he sent to Jennies solicitors. He copied each and every item he sent, and each and every item that was sent dealt with the alleged incidents.

It transpired that the 'proof' was the fact that myself and Jane had been alone in the room when the alleged incident took place. And of course, she was far too young to offer an opinion, to this day she still cannot remember the incident.

So in essence, Jennies relative had all of the 'proof' she needed, whilst not been substantiated by anybody, the authorities took one look at the incident, and had taken it upon themselves to accuse me of using violence in the most vile way against my daughter.

At this point in time, I truly felt like giving up, but it was only through my father's intervention that I carried on fighting to some degree. A fight that I was bound to lose in the long run, but a fight that was needed.

Further on down the line Nigel rang me and asked me to go and see him in his office. The normal pleasantries were exchanged, coffee and tea partaken, and it was this time that Nigel told me the news.

I don't know if anybody else has been in this position, but it was one I found myself in. Basically, Nigel informed me that in law I 'should' have full access to my children, but unfortunately the law isn't always the same as 'justice'. He then went on to say that I stood absolutely no chance of forcing the other parties involved to let me see my children.

I was after all, a man who had used 'violence' against his daughter, and the courts of the land would not take kindly to me having access to my children with the threat of this hanging over them. Nigel's exact words were, 'Ryan, if you push this too far you will not see your children within the next six months, maybe a year, if you insist on fighting what has been said, you will end up losing and making yourself ill'.

In other words what Nigel had said to me was simply this. I did not have a cat in hells chance of seeing my children until the other solicitors deemed fit. If I did take it upon myself to try and see my children a restraining order would be taken out against me and I could be arrested, as in Nigel's words, 'You are deemed a threat not only to your children, but also your estranged wife'.

After I had tried to assimilate this information I asked Nigel exactly what I was meant to do, and I received an answer that I did not think possible. He basically said that I needed to walk away from the situation and let things calm down a bit before any attempt was made to communicate with both Jennie and my kids.

Of course I took this on board, but the threat of arrest was not going to stop me from seeing my children. I had been lied about, and my character assassinated in the simple declaration that I used violence against my eldest daughter. I decided to try and talk to Jennie personally over the telephone. This was an action that I lived to regret.

Each and every time I would try to make contact with Jennie the phone would be put down on me, or worse, I would be screamed and shouted at. I had no idea why this situation had snowballed so quickly, but I was adamant that I would try to see my kids as much as possible.

I tried on numerous occasions to talk to Jennie and make her see some kind of sense. But was each and every time ignored, and I never had the chance to talk to her about what was going on. I had my suspicions at this time about who was the instigator of the lies that were circulating, but to prove such a thing was impossible.

They were a so called member of a select group of individuals who had businesses in the local area and many people looked up to them, they never really knew the real person, they just saw a business person who was, yes, I agree, very successful, but one of the cruelest people I have ever met.

It was basically their word against mine, and I stood no chance. It was at this stage that I did something very, very silly indeed. I decided to go around to Jennies house and demand to see my children. It was a decision that yet again was to haunt me for many months to come.

I arrived at around 7:30 p.m at Jennies address, with my heart in my mouth I knocked on the door and hoped, indeed prayed, that I would be met with some degree of courtesy and civility. Nothing could be further from the truth.

I think I just about managed to utter these words, 'Hello, how are', when Jennie informed me, or rather screamed at me if I did not go away she would phone the police. At this point in time my frustration boiled over, and my anger came out in a very inappropriate way. There had always been a dog basket down by the side entrance to the house, in my anger I kicked the dog basket, which cracked the plastic surround around the side.

That is all I did, nothing else. I admit it was a silly thing to do, but after all, I just wanted to talk to Jennie and hope she would listen to a little of what I wanted to say. I thought, however foolishly that I would be met with a modicum of civility.

I walked away at this point in time as I still had enough mental capacity to realise what I had done, and it was best if I left the premises as soon as possible to stop the situation escalating.

However, the very next morning I received a telephone call from Nigel saying that the police had been informed of my actions and they would be coming round later to take a statement.

I said to Nigel all I had done was kick the dog basket, his reply was simple in essence. Apparently I had tried to kick Jennie and force my way into the house to see my children. Unbeknown to me the evening I had gone round to see Jennie the relative in question was in the living room and had fabricated this story to give her more so called 'evidence' to use against me.

Yes, I admit that the actions I took that night were not at all appropriate, but they were actions born out of sheer frustration and sadness. I had never, and have never used physical against any member of the fairer sex, let alone against any members of my own sex.

I have on occasion been in a situation when I was younger when I did use my fists in anger, but this was some thirty odd years ago, and since that time I have not taken such a path. School yard punch ups, more akin to handbags at dawn, nothing more, nothing less. I can in all honesty say that since I was about fifteen I have never used physical against anybody or anything.

Several more communications took place between myself and Nigel before the police arrived at my door. I was escorted to the police station where I had to give a signed statement of my version of events that evening. I have no idea if the police looked upon my version of events as the truth, when all was said and done that is all I could do, give my account of the events.

As time went by Nigel and myself had many conversations revolving around my rights to see my children. But, in reality I stood no chance of seeing my children for the foreseeable future unless it was deemed right and proper by the appropriate authorities, and the appropriate authorities seemed to be listening to a certain member of Jennies family above all others. I was for all intents and purposes now of no use to anybody, apart from those that I had around me.

To see the justice system work in this manner is truly shocking. As far as I was concerned my marriage had broken down, very sad and tense for all those involved. But at the end of the day that's all it was, a marriage break down that can in the long-term be gotten over with the love and support of those around you. I just wanted to make sure that Jennie was still OK, and to be able to see my children once again.

By this time I was at a place in my life where I truly did not know which way to turn next. I was at a loss as to what to do for the best. Nigel had made it very obvious that I had little recourse to use the law in order for me to have access to my children.

The allegations against me were so virulent and spiteful that any hope of seeing my children in the near future were minimal indeed. Looking back at this time I can now say that the law was right to a certain degree.

If they think that a child's welfare may be at risk, no matter how small that risk, then they should be able to exercise their right to protect that child. This I have to agree with. But I had done nothing wrong at this time, and to me, the law was indeed an 'ass'.

I had by this time lost some three and a half stone in weight. I had always been a constant weight of around thirteen stone, not huge, but certainly not small. I had now reached a weight of just under nine and a half stone. My cloths hung of me, and I looked truly dreadful.

I was not sleeping at all well, and my whole demeanour was one of abject disillusionment and despondency. I never believed in troubling doctors too much, but my parents at this time were insistent that I seek some kind of medical intervention.

For my parents sake I booked an appointment with my local doctor in the hope that they could help, or at the very least put my parents minds at rest. I knew that there was no magic wand that they could wave that would make my life any better, but in some way I hoped that they could give me something to make me try and forget a little of what was going on. I had never been one for tablets or pills, but I hoped that maybe my doctor could give me some advice.

My doctor was a man of few words, but the words he did utter were always ones of great depth and wisdom in their meaning. At the time I did not appreciate what he said, but now I can look back at this time and appreciate what he was trying to tell me.

At no point in time did he offer me any kind of medication. No tablets, pills, potions or miracle cures. All he said to me was this, 'This is going to be one of the worst times of your life. At times things will seem as though there is no reason to carry on. But I can assure you that you will now see and do things that you thought impossible once upon a time. I am not speaking of sex, or anything like that. What I am saying is this. That you know find yourself in a position that you have little control over, you will have to adapt to being a different person. And in becoming a different person you will as I have said, witness and do things that you would of never done in your life before. You will come through this I can assure you, but it takes time. You have to have something in your life that is yours, and yours alone. You have to have a goal that you aim and strive for.'

At that time I didn't really understand what he was trying to say to me. And at certain times when he was speaking to me I wanted to throttle him. How dare he say these things to me? All I wanted was my family back. But here he was, telling me that I had to become a 'different' person and experience things that I could not imagine, nor in point of fact, wanted.

All I wanted to do was experience the warmth and love of my family once again. To have them around me and loving me as once they had. But one thing did shine through that he was saying to me. He had told me that I had to have a goal, something that was mine and mine alone.

To me this meant one thing, Australia. It had always been a place dear to my heart and something that was for the most part, mine. It is true, that at times other people had shared Australia with me, but in reality Australia had always been with me, and my relationship with this country was one that is difficult to explain.

It is also true that I had blamed Australia in no small measure for the breakdown of my marriage. But even this was not enough to diminish my love and affection for the country and its people. Australia had always been with me, in mind, body and spirit, and it was now, when I was in the very deepest recesses of depression that I needed her to get me through once again.

I made the decision to return to Australia and hopefully get my life back on some sort of track. It was blatantly obvious that I had no chance of seeing my children in the near future, and this was reason enough for me to disappear to Australia once again to try and sort my life out.

I was left with little choice. I had done all I could to try and ease the situation between myself and Jennie, but this had been to no avail. All I wanted was for Jennie and my children to be happy in some way.

I would do all I could to enable this to happen. If I were completely truthful whilst I wanted to get away from the stress and torment I was feeling, there was a bigger reason why I decided once again to travel back to Australia.

I honestly thought that if I was no longer in the picture causing all kinds of trouble, or so I thought, then maybe, just maybe, Jennie and my young family would once again get back on an even keel and hopefully find someone who could obviously make them far happier than I ever had.

I truly felt a deeply entrenched sense of responsibility to my family. If I could only stay away for a period of time then I was sure that they would all be far better off, in the long-term. It was obvious that I had never made them truly happy, so I thought that if Jennie could find someone else to love then they would all be OK after all.

That sounds as if I was feeling sorry for myself. Nothing could be further from the truth. I have never been one to wallow in self pity. All I thought was that maybe with me out of the picture they would all one day, find true happiness.

After much discussion and heart searching I made the decision to once again travel back to Australia. However, I did have one last request that I wanted to ask Jennie. I knew only too well that if I just turned up on Jennies doorstep I would be met with aggression and anger, so I took it upon myself to write her a letter.

My request was simple in the extreme. I asked that before

I leave for Australia I was allowed to see my children one last time before I went. I fully expected that this letter would be met with negativity, but to my surprise Jennie said that I should go to their house and say goodbye to the kids.

I realised this was going to be one of the hardest things I had ever done, but I not only owed it to my children, and Jennie to some degree, but owed it to myself in no small measure. So I took the decision to go to the house the Sunday before I travelled.

It was a warm sultry day when I arrived, the approach to the front door was full of dread and excitement. After all, I hadn't seen my children for nearly three months. Would they still recognise me? Would they hate me? I had no idea about the reception I was going to receive.

I knocked on the front door and was asked to come in by Jennie. The only words that were spoken were the niceties. Jennie said to me that if I wanted, I could take the children out as it was a nice day, and maybe we could go to the park.

As my children came down the stairs I could see by their faces that they were pleased to see me. Hugs and laughter soon followed and we decided that we would indeed travel to the park to get an ice cream.

We sat on the grassy bank and soon enough the inevitable questions came about. My children, still very young had no real idea what had taken place during the last few months. In their innocence they believed that any problems we had as a family could easily be rectified.

We could all kiss and make up and everything would return to normal. I did my best to explain to them the situation, but I feel I fell somewhat short. How do you explain to two young children that as adults we make mistakes, and for all intense and purposes mess up our lives and hurt all those around us?

I did my very best to explain, but in the cold light of day I do not think that my explanation was good enough. At no point in time did I apportion blame. To do so would have been most unfair. I just tried my hardest to say that me and their mum, though still loving each other very much, could no longer live together.

I also tried to explain to them my reasons for going back to Australia. To them they must have been empty and cowardly reasons, and I guess in no small measure they were right, but nonetheless I did my very best.

As I have said previously, I have no great belief in faith, but this one time that I truly wish I did. I wanted to pray to a God and ask them for their guidance and advice. In reality it was down to me to try and explain the situation, and I fell somewhat short.

I took the children back to the house early that evening. I had made a pact with myself that I would not cry in front of them, and I did indeed keep to that promise I made to myself, until a certain point.

I said to them that if they ever missed me that they should look up to the sky and ask God to let me hear them. I assured them that no matter what, God would pass their message onto me and I would be able to hear their voices even though I was many miles away.

It was at this point in time that the emotion I felt was truly sickening. It was all I could do to hold the tears back. My voice was breaking, and my head pounding. Tears started to fall from my face, and there was little I could about it.

By this time both my children were now in tears and they collapsed into my arms and just sobbed their hearts out. I did all I could to ensure that they knew how much I loved them and always would, but at that point in time all I felt was a failure, an abject failure of a husband and dad.

To say goodbye to your children not knowing when you will see them again is a feeling that I have not since experienced, thank God. I cannot possibly put into words just how I felt on this day.

The pervading atmosphere by this time was one of great sadness and grief, there is no other way of describing it. By this time Jennie was standing in the kitchen, back to me, looking out to the rear garden. As I got up from hugging my children and without looking around all she said to me was 'Sorry'.

At that moment in my life all I wanted to do was go over to her and hold her, and tell her everything was alright. But I knew deep down that this would have been wrong. It would not only have confused the children, but also would have been totally inappropriate.

The reason for Jennie saying sorry were as clear as day. Though I did not expect, or indeed want an apology, Jennie was in her own way trying to explain to me that what had happened was no bodies fault and hopefully we would all come through this.

I had at this point asked my children to go upstairs as there were certain things that I needed to say to their mum. All I said to Jennie was that I hoped and prayed that she would be OK, and hopefully she would one day find happiness with someone else.

Jennie never commented on this. I could tell that tears were falling from her cheeks, and little I said or did would have been any comfort to her at this point in time. As I turned and went to make my exit I remember seeing Jennie fall to her knees and sob uncontrollably.

The journey back to my parents house was normally some forty minutes in duration, on this occasion it took nearly four hours for me to get there. I drove to a local church and just sat in the car park. As I have said many times I have little faith in any so called 'God' but at this precise moment in time I truly wanted a 'God' to hear me.

For hours I screamed at the top of my voice how 'F.....G' cruel' God was, and then in the next breath asked him for the strength to carry on. Obviously I was not thinking straight, but all I wanted was a sign that Jennie and the children would be alright and they would one day, find true happiness.

I apologised to 'God' for being such a bad human being and asked that he immediately tell me what to do next? I was convinced at this stage in my life that life was no longer worth living, and if it was so deemed that my life ended now, so that all those around me would eventually be alright, then so be it.

To say that I was in the depths of despair does in no way do the situation justice. I was not thinking rationally or sanely. All I wanted to know was that all those that I loved and cared about would be OK. I was at this time convinced that my mere existence had done so much harm that for me to carry on living was a disgrace.

Somehow I managed to get myself back to my parents house and was as ever surrounded with the love and comfort of my parents. Nothing they said or did at this time made me feel any better, but the mere fact that they were there was enough to convince me that I had to carry on.

Obviously once in Australia I would have to leave a forwarding address, of which I had none, as I truly had no idea where I was going to go, or what I was going to do. All I knew was that at this stage in my life I needed to get out to Australia, come what may.

Even now, at one of the worst points in my life, my main concern was Jennies welfare and my children's. I must admit that at times the feeling of hatred and resentment was overpowering, but the vast majority of the time I wanted to know that Jennie was going to be OK, and my children would be looked after in the best possible way.

The 'Retreat'. Peace!
****

It was early March when I decided to travel back to Australia, I was going to go back to Cairns, a place that I knew well and one that had welcomed me with open arms before. However, this time I decided that I would firstly travel to Sydney, then make my way up the east coast to Cairns.

I had no real idea why I made this decision. Maybe it was the need to arrive in a large and bustling city in the hope that I could in some way get lost and maybe become anonymous amongst the throngs of people. Maybe it was the need to delay the arrival into Cairns, as this city had many memories attached to it, both good and bad.

But all I knew at this point in time was the need for some kind of perspective in my life. In reality I was at a complete loss as to what I was, and who I was. I had been a dad and a husband, now this had been taken from me and I truly had no idea what I was meant to do, or indeed 'be' next.

My parents at this time pleaded with me not to go as they thought I could be looked after far better back in the UK, but I was adamant that I had to go in order for my life to have some semblance of normality, if this was at all possible.

I was not at this time what you would call mentally capable of looking after myself, but I was adamant in my decision to go back to Australia. My mind at this time was full of every conceivable emotion. At times I would be in the depths of despair, at absolute rock bottom, and at other times I would be as high as a kite, full of thoughts about how my future would pan out and the possibilities that lay ahead. But these thoughts would soon come down to earth with a bump. I was after all, utterly confused as to what my future held.

I had by this time taken a job at a local bakery. As I wasn't sleeping well at night I thought it best if I take employment during my darkest hours as this may keep my mind occupied.

I would rise from bed at 3 a.m and make the short walk

down to the bakery. My working day was from 3:45 a.m till 11 a.m. The job, whilst being fairly enjoyable and active still in no way could ever fill the void I was now feeling.

The pay was the minimum that would allow, but it still enabled me to save a little money for my trip back to Australia. My only intention at this time was to try and in some way regain a little sanity in the hope that I could once again start to rebuild my now shattered life.

My parents at this time as you would imagine were extremely worried about me and virtually begged me not to go back. After all, they thought that they could look after me only too well. In truth I knew that they would be able to do such a thing. But I also knew that Australia would in her own indomitable way look 'after me' also.

The day finally dawned that a return to Australia was once again upon me. My father took to the airport me on a chilly and damp March morning. There are only two occasions that I have ever seen my father cry, and this was one of them. I did not know what to say or do, all I knew was that the quicker I got Australia the quicker I may be able to return with my head sorted out.

All I had with me was one very small carry on bag that contained the necessities of life, change of clothes, wash bag, and a couple of hundred Australian dollars. That was all I needed, after all I was now trying to start over again, and the less baggage I had the better.

I checked in as normal, and went through the departure gate a lot earlier than I would have done normally, as all I wanted was to set foot on the aircraft and get to Australia once again as soon as possible.

Bearing in mind that my sanity at this time was seriously in doubt then I hope you can appreciate a little of what I had to cope with.

My mind at this time was all over the place and very rarely did I have a rational train of thought. There are a few moments in ones life that are deeply embedded in one owns psyche. Normally these thoughts and emotions are there when we are on a relative level plain, and often such memories are held very close to us.

However, I was not at all what you could call rational at this point in my life, and there are two memories that still to this day are as vivid today as they were then.

Firstly, whilst I was sitting in the departure hall I could have sworn that I heard Jennie, Jane, and Betty coming up the escalators asking me to stay. It was as if it was actually happening to me, as if my family had somehow changed their minds about the situation and they all wanted me back.

I honestly thought I heard both Jane and Betty shout my name and asked me to stay. As I turned around to look where the voices came from there was nothing, absolutely nothing. Just ordinary people, doing ordinary things. No wife, no children shouting my name and asking me to stay. Nothing, nothing at all.

The second experience was as vivid as the first. As is the norm when you board the aircraft some of us pick up the in-flight magazine that is in the inside pocket in front of each seat. It is true that more often than not such magazines are often full of expensive and useless paraphernalia, but we often try to take our minds off the flight ahead by reading such material.

I had boarded the aircraft, and as usual started to flick through one of the many magazines that was in front of me. I often did this, as it not only negated boredom setting in, but also whiled away the time until the aircraft took off and I could once again fall asleep.

I flicked through the programme guide that detailed what was going to be screened for my viewing pleasure, and also the duty free section that showed what was available to purchase on the flight. In amongst the many items there was a gift set of rather expensive perfumes.

I remember saying to myself that I will have to buy these while on the aircraft as this sort of thing would appeal to Jennie, it was as if nothing had happened previously, and she was still with me, and this gift would have made her smile. But that was not the case, within seconds of this thought process I was jarred back into the cold light of day and the realisation that I was daydreaming. I put this thought down to circumstances, and in no time at all I was once again faced with the fact I was by myself.

The flight as ever to Australia was long and time consuming. But as normal within an hour of the flight taking off I was fast asleep. This time though it was through exhaustion, not the motion of the aircraft.

I arrived in Sydney at 7:15 a.m on a Friday afternoon, as I said, I had no idea where I was going to go or stay, but I have always been a fairly resilient character and was not worried in the slightest.

Once through customs and immigration I proceeded to the main airport terminal where the first port of call was the nearest coffee outlet. I purchased the largest coffee available and went straight outside to light my first cigarette. I know it's a disgusting habit, and one that I have often longed to give up, but unless you are a smoker it is impossible to imagine the joy that this first cigarette brings after the long flight from the UK.

I still had no idea where, or what I was going to do, but knew that my limited funds would only feed and cloth me for a limited time, so in order to save as much money as I could I went to the taxi rank and asked to be taken to the cheapest accommodation available. The taxi driver as normal asked exactly what I meant, and I told him of my circumstances and explained that as long as the accommodation was close to the city that would suit me fine.

After what seemed an eternity I arrived at my port of call. I don't know how many of you know Sydney that well, but where I had arrived at was rather a shock. The taxi driver explained to me that this area was one of the cheaper areas of Sydney and should suit me just fine. It transpired that I had been dropped off in Kings Cross.

Bearing in mind that I didn't know Sydney that well I had

no idea of what lay ahead of me. By this time all I wanted was a bed where I could relax and hopefully chill out for a while. I walked into the first available hotel that I saw and was greeted by a rather robust lady who welcomed me with what can only be described as complete distain. Her demeanour was one of disengagement and complete ignorance.

However, little that she said or did had any great impact on me. After all, I had just stepped of a very long flight and as far as I was concerned, little she said or did had any relevance to my life.

I awoke the next morning, still rather dazed and confused. Not to put too a finer point on it, I was for all intense and purposes in the mindset of an individual who could not care less what happened to himself, and I was rather dejected.

It was only at this time that the full scale of my new accommodation hit me. The bed had seen far better days, stains and an odd, rather musty smell emanated from the mattress, and it was all I could do to convince myself that I had slept in the bloody thing that night.

The décor was what can only be described as 'minimal' in its appearance. Wall paper hanging from the walls, and the ceiling had obviously been bombed at some stage by stray Japanese fighter plane.

If I thought that the interior of the hotel was somewhat shocking I had yet to venture outside. Kings Cross was, as it is now, one of Sydney's more bizarre suburbs. Upon first look you could compare it to Soho, London. Seedy sex shops, down-market souvenir establishments, and bars and clubs of a rather dubious appearance and nature.

I am very broad minded, but even I was somewhat shocked and aghast at what lay before me. However, after taking the time to assimilate what was before me it soon became apparent that this 'community' had a friendly and welcoming nature.

I would often take myself off in the evening and just walk

for hours at a time around the streets of Kings Cross. The characters and things I saw are for another time, but the situations I found myself in have led in no small part to the man I now am.

It was obvious that I would soon have to move on. I was beginning to question my own sanity once again as I found myself wanting more and more to become a part of the community I know found myself in. But I realised that I was left with little choice but to move on, and hopefully find a goal once more.

With this in mind I booked myself a greyhound coach ticket to Cairns which was due to leave in four days time. This period would give me time to hopefully get ready to face Cairns once again. I still thought of Cairns as my home, only this time it was without my family around me. I hoped that if I could in someway face Cairns again, then maybe I would be able to get myself back on track.

I boarded the coach a few days later with trepidation and excitement. A strange mixture maybe, but all I knew at this time was the need for some clarity and a goal in my new life. The coach journey would last approximately two days and would give me the opportunity to see parts of Australia that I had only read about, and knew little of.

Whilst the journey was arduous and tiring I did have the pleasure of sitting next to a young man from America by the name of Wayne. Now Wayne was a very nice, polite, and respectful individual who had many positive attributes. But there was one problem.

It transpired that he was a born again christian and had been sent to Australia by his church back in the USA to spend some time in their affiliate churches on the east coast of Australia. I am not what you could describe a christian. I sometimes believe there is a greater being than us, a spirit if you will, but I very rarely pondered the bigger questions of our time, up too this point.

For the whole two days Wayne insisted on talking to me

about all things religious. His conversation was incessant and to some extent mind numbingly boring. I have never been one to be rude to anyone, and this was not going to be any different. I tried my best to act interested, and in some way not offend him. He was after all, not going out of his way to offend me.

It would be lie to say that Wayne made me into a better person. But in some very small measure I guess he did, I learnt that even though I may not agree with all he said I still had the courtesy and politeness to not offend him. If truth were known we became fairly close over those two days, however not close enough that I didn't want to say goodbye to Wayne as soon as possible.

We arrived in Cairns on a warm and sultry afternoon. Nothing had really changed in any great detail. The same buildings, smells, and features were still there. But this was different. I no longer had the comfort of my family around me, and this was something that I would have to get used to, very quickly.

I booked into a motel that was in the heart of the city, as I thought this would allow me the convenience of being close to the employment opportunities. However, after only a few short days it was obvious that my money was not going to last that long and I would have to find cheaper accommodation as soon as possible.

With this in mind I looked in the yellow pages and happened across an advert for a backpackers conveniently named 'The Retreat'. The ad said the retreat was set amongst the rainforest and was indeed a retreat away from civilisation. I made a phone call and was told by a young lad that I would be picked up from my hotel the very next morning by his father, door to door service if you will.

The next day dawned and true to their word at 8:30 a.m there was a knock at my door. I don't know what I was expecting, but it certainly wasn't what was before me. A rather short, bearded gentlemen stood before me with a massive grin on his face, and a, 'G'day Ryan, you ready'?

The journey to the backpackers accommodation was only about half an hour and it was one of the most memorable journeys I have ever had. Not at any point did 'Col' try to strike up any kind of conversation or relationship. Now this may have come across as rude to some people, but Col was a true Queenslander, laid back, and extremely affable, it was only later that I was to realise what impact Col and the 'retreat' would have on the rest of my life.

As we drove toward Palm Cove it truly took my breath away. The scenery was, as it is now, spectacular, rainforest on the left and ocean on the right, it truly was a sight to take your breath away.

Having arrived in Palm Cove we proceeded to turn left up a dirt track that seemed to lead nowhere. After a few minutes we turned a corner and there before me stood what I can only describe as my refuge.

This was no ordinary backpackers. Set among some of the most beautiful and spectacular scenery I had ever seen. The rainforest literally swallowed up the accommodation, and if you didn't know the retreat was there you would never find it in a million years.

It was basically eight cabins, all joined together to make one long row, only separated by the kitchen area and general purpose living area. I knew from this moment in time I would be OK, in the long run, or so I thought.

The retreat seemed to have an aura about it. I couldn't quite put my finger on it. It was a feeling of peace and tranquility. At first glance the accommodation seemed basic and rather sparse, but this was offset by the magnificent scenery that surrounded it. The sounds emanating from the rainforest, even though strange and unfamiliar, immediately made me feel comforted and settled.

As we all do when we first arrive somewhere new and meet new people we are fairly tentative in our first meeting with these people. As I hope you will be aware I was in a rather fragile state at this stage and really did not want to have to meet too many people with a fixed grin on my face.

Col took me to my room which was shared accommodation, and as I walked in I knew I had arrived in a very special place indeed. The accommodation was made up of two bunk beds, and one very small writing desk, the barest of necessities, but after all, that is all I needed.

The retreat was by no means full at this point in time, so fortunately I only had to share with one other person. If I'd known then what I know now I would have done things a little differently.

My comrade in arms as it were, was a gentleman by the name of 'Kiwi', a New Zealander who was very quick to introduce himself, may I add rather forcefully. I was to realise the depths of my dilemma in a short while.

The retreat as I've said was by no means full, but there were a number of people staying near, some Aussies, some Brits and a few other Europeans. I guess it was around sixty percent full, with a mixed age range of between seventeen years old, to my new comrade in arms (kiwi), who must have been approaching his sixties.

It soon transpired that the retreat was in some way a refuge for all those who had some personal problems. Why this was the case I couldn't tell you. I am not a particularly religious man, nor did I believe in anything like faith, or in essence any kind of spirituality. But I believe in my heart of hearts that in someway, shape or form something guided me towards the retreat during my stay in Cairns.

Each and every individual who I spoke to was having some kind of emotional crisis. I know it is hard to believe, and I wouldn't have believed it if I hadn't seen it with my own eyes. The range of people there were as mixed and as varied as you would ever want to meet.

As I have said, I have changed certain names in the vast majority of cases throughout this book not only to protect the individuals themselves, but also to protect myself. I would dearly love to use peoples real names, particularly in this chapter, as the people at the retreat truly did become my salvation. But to name them would not only be unfair, but I know only too well that their modesty would be jeopardised if I took this course of action.

After some rather tentative introductions to all those staying at the retreat I soon began to feel at home. The retreat had an atmosphere of serenity and community spirit. It is extremely difficult to put into words the atmosphere of the retreat. To this day I have never felt anything like it, and if truth were known I hope I never do.

It was a time in my life that was very dear to me, and if I were to feel this atmosphere of serenity again in my life I feel it would in some way diminish what I experienced. There are often moments in one's life that are unique, and this was one of those occasions. If I were to experience such feelings again in someway I feel as though I was being somewhat treacherous.

There was one particular lady there who I am indebted to for the rest of my life. I cannot, and will not specify too much about her, but if she ever gets to read this book I hope she realises the impact she had on my life. She was a lady in her mid-fifties who had arrived at the retreat because of a very difficult situation back in her homeland of South Africa.

I don't know if she saw in me a need for human contact, or just saw me as someone who needed some comfort. From the very minute I met her she was an inspiration to me, and if it were not for her I know I would not be here today.

We would spend hours just talking about everything under the sun. From politics to sport, any subject at all. Whilst the age gap between us was some twenty years we just seemed to have so much in common.

From the very moment I met her I knew that I had found a true friend. I had always been very independent when it came to trying to look after myself. I cooked, ironed and laundered for myself, but 'Jo' would hear little of it. It was as if she was mothering me. I was not allowed to do anything for myself. She would cook, wash my clothes and look after me to an extent that was rather shocking, bearing in mind I hardly knew this lady.

When I was at my lowest ebb all she would do was to put her arms around me and hold me. She would not say a word, at all. Just hold me and wait for my pain to go away. To this day I cannot thank her enough for what she did, and said.

All in all each and every resident of the retreat had in someway a form of emotional trauma that they were trying to get over. Now I am not for one minute trying to excuse or exonerate what happened within the next two or three months, there is nothing I can do to change the past, it happened and that is something that I have learned to deal with.

But because of the emotional trauma that seemed to be all around me, and bearing in mind the physical and emotional wreck that I was, I and others around me were looking for some type of release valve, and that release valve happened to be alcohol.

There are many of us enjoy who a drink and can control such drinking. I still include myself in this category, or at least I do now, at that time, alcohol did play a big part in my life.

I never woke craving alcohol, and I could function quite easily without alcohol, but my alcohol consumption was what you would call 'excessive', and at times the demon drink did get a hold of me. I was not what you would call an alcoholic, not by any stretch of the imagination, but alcohol did start to play a hugely significant part in my life.

It wasn't just me, each of us at the retreat would use alcohol to in some way try and blot out the memories of what we were going through. It would be easy to judge me, and others around me, but until you have been in this situation please withhold judgement and try to understand a little of what was going through my head.

I had for all intents and purposes lost utterly and completely what I was as a human being. My wife and children had through no fault of my own been taken from me, and there was little I could do to get them back in the near future.

Each and every morning I would wake not knowing who I was, what I was meant to be doing, and where I was going to go in life. My wife and children had been my very existence, they were what I breathed, ate, drank, and slept. They were indeed my life, now they were gone I truly had no idea of what I was meant to be any more.

So with that said, I hope you can sympathise to some degree why I found comfort in alcohol, it numbed to some degree the pain that I was feeling, and I admit openly, helped me get through each day. I realise that this is not a good thing to say, but it is true nonetheless.

I had been in Australia approximately two months, I had now lost four and a half stone in weight, and I was surviving on a certain brand of potato chips and literally litres of alcohol. Jo would cook me as many meals as she could, but I would often disappear for hours at a time wandering around in the rainforest.

Often at these times I would reflect on my previous life, for now that's exactly what it was, a previous life. The life, or rather existence that I was now leading was wholly different. Yes, the alcohol did numb the pain and grief to some degree, but these were the briefest of moments. All too soon I would be jolted back to reality and the devastation I felt had not dissipated in anyway.

I would make calls back to the UK regularly, not only to talk to my parents, but also to try and talk to Jennie and my two children. Unfortunately, each and every time I tried to speak to Jennie the phone would ring off the hook, or if someone did answer the phone it would be put straight back down again once my voice was heard.

I was doing my best to maintain contact with both my children, but this was to no avail. So I would once again find comfort in the bottom of a bottle in the vain hope this would nullify the feelings I was having. This would work for several hours, then the effects of the alcohol would start to wear off and I would be back where I started, so once again I would consume vast amounts of alcohol to keep me going.

My parents at this time could not have been more worried. Though I tried to pacify them with my conversation I have little doubt they knew otherwise. I would speak in glowing terms of how I was doing, that my life now had some direction and meaning. But deep down I knew that whatever I said was looked upon rather suspiciously by my ever loving parents.

Jo as always was a true friend. I found her an excellent listener, and she could not only sympathise, but also empathise with my situation. We would sit up for hours and hours just talking, not only about our emotional traumas, but also about many other subjects, in actual fact, at times, we would put the world to rights.

As with any marriage breakup there are always those that say, 'There's plenty more fish in the sea', 'Every cloud has a silver lining', or many cliches along those lines. I realise that all they are trying to do is help, but at times these sort of cliches just want to make you scream that all you want back is your old life.

Jo never did this. She would just listen and whenever she could, try and comfort me. I hope that one day I will be able to repay her kindness. Somehow I doubt it, as the debt is too enormous to even contemplate paying back.

New Love
****

I dare say from an outsider's point of view, I would have been classed at this time as an emotional wreck. And I guess, I was, if I were truly honest with myself I was indeed a complete and utter physical and emotional wreck.

This is going to sound odd to say, but all I wanted was someone to tell me that I wasn't a bad person, that I was worthy of someone loving me, and I guess I just needed someone to show me that I had a future. I would have clung to anything at this stage in my life, absolutely anything that made me feel that I had a future.

I was at this time not one to believe in a rebound relationship. After all, how on earth could you build a relationship with someone else when you still crave an old relationship you had? But, at this stage I would have had any kind of relationship, purely because it would have meant that I wasn't a bad person after all.

It was mid october when a young lady by the name of Susie appeared at the retreat. She was english, gorgeous, and shared my sense of humour, which by this point in time had become rather sarcastic and skeptical.

Susie was eight years younger than myself and it transpired she travelling around Australia on a years working visa. She was open, honest, and she seemed extremely easy to talk to. To say I was not attracted to her would be a lie, but I was extremely attracted to not only her looks, but her whole demeanour.

Now bearing in mind that it had only been eight months since myself and Jennie had separated some would say that I was on the rebound, and so emotionally shallow that I would of jumped on the first woman I saw.

Neither of the above statements are true, I just wanted, and needed, someone to tell me I would be OK, and that I did have a future. Myself and Susie got on really well, though it must be admitted that at times, our alcohol consumption was truly awesome, so maybe that's why we got on so well. That's an unfair statement to make. We truly did click the minute we saw each other, and to say otherwise is completely wrong.

But we did hit it off the minute we met, and I can also say with hand on heart I never had any intentions of starting up yet another relationship. Nothing could be further from the truth, all I wanted was my wife and children back, and if I could have had this then I would have returned to the UK as soon as possible. But I guess I'd come to a realisation that this was never going to be the case, so I had better try and make the best of a very bad situation.

From the previous correspondence I had not only from Nigel, my solicitor, but also my family and friends, it was very obvious that the marriage between myself and Jennie had gone beyond repair, there was never a chance that a reconciliation would be possible, by any stretch of the imagination.

I remember my birthday in Cairns, it was one of the lowest points of my life, if it could have got any lower. I received two birthday cards from my children. Col used to bring the post around every morning and handed it out in the communal area. Now this is going to sound extremely harsh, but I hoped and prayed that I would never receive any birthday cards from anyone, let alone my children.

It just served as a reminder, yet again, that I had two young children back in the UK that I was not allowed to see, or even contact. On the morning in question I received two letters, and from the postmark I immediately knew who they were from. I took the cards and walked down to beach, which was around a twenty minute stroll.

I sat on the end of a jetty and opened the cards. For at least ten minutes I couldn't make out a word that was written, my eyes were full of tears and my body shaking to a degree that it hasn't shaken before, or since.

I still have the cards with me today, and they serve as a

reminder of where I was at this particular time in my life. They are indeed, a constant reminder that my life at that time had no meaning, and was never likely to.

I would often chat to Susie about my situation and even though I think she found it difficult to comprehend, by the mere fact that she just listened, she helped me immensely.

I had by this time become extremely close to Susie, I was not trying to substitute my children, after all my children were my world and they could never be substituted. But what I had found in Susie was a person who was caring, loving, and above all, someone who could support me and show me their support by the bucket load.

As I've said, I have never been one to believe in love on the rebound, and to even contemplate that this was the situation with me and Susie would not do it justice. I had in my own mind become accustomed to knowing that myself and Jennie would never be together again.

I apologise if this does sound harsh, but in all honesty when these things happen to you your mind can at times play tricks. I had in essence put Jennie in a box, locked the box, and put this box somewhere in my mind that I could never access it again. That was the only way I could cope with what was going on with me, it was all I could do each and everyday to rise each morning knowing that I no longer had my family with me.

I guess what I'm trying to say is simply this. That we are all different, we all deal with such emotional trauma in a way that makes us survive as individuals, and my survival instinct was to block Jennie away somewhere where I would never think about her, and hopefully this would make me whole again.

My children of course, were a completely different scenario. I had come to the conclusion over many weeks and months that to try and fight the situation back in the UK would inevitably lead to the children's unhappiness. If I were to take extreme legal measures and fight the access situation to my children then it was obvious that this would impact on my children's lives.

I realised I was not going to be a part of their lives in the near future, and if I was to push the matter of access to the limit it would only impact on them. I can honestly say, and again this is going to sound harsh, but somehow I managed to convince myself that the children were no longer part of me.

I used to be classed as a dad, now I was classed as a 'father'. In essence, in my own mind, I had managed to fully convince myself that even though I had helped bring my children into the world I was going to play no future role in their upbringing, except for the fact that I would send them money regularly in the hope that it would help them somewhat.

I am finding this extremely difficult to explain, and I realise I am coming over extremely hard, and harsh. It was a switch that had been switched on in my brain. A switch that had told me that I was no longer a 'dad'. I had no control over this switch, none whatsoever.

Subconsciously my brain had managed to overcome any logical thought process, and it had convinced me that my two children were better off without me in their lives. It was a form of self-preservation, and ultimately, survival.

At times I imagine we all have this instinct. Where to try to comprehend or even think about a very painful moment in our lives is to awful to contemplate. So somewhere in the very darkest recesses of our minds we manage to put away such thoughts in order for us to survive, no matter how tenuously.

All of this I hope you can understand, and in so doing understand what happened next. Susie, as she was on a working holiday visa was going to make the most of her stay in Australia, and for this reason she had pre-booked a coach trip to Darwin. Now we had only known each other for a matter of weeks but I decided I would tell her exactly what I thought of our relationship.

I wrote Susie a letter and tried explain to her exactly how I felt, and hopefully it would help her come to a decision. The letter

I wrote was really a double edged sword. In one way I wrote the letter and really did spill my guts to her about how I felt, and on the other hand I let her know that I truly was an emotional wreck, and I was not a fit person to enter into any type of long-term relationship.

I hoped by doing this that it would have driven her away, for two reasons. Firstly, was the fact that even though deep down I wanted to be loved, and indeed, to love, the thought of being hurt again truly did make me feel sick, and secondly I wanted her to realise what she meant to me.

Once again, it is very difficult to put into words just what I felt at this time. All I knew was that I had found someone that hopefully, in the future I could build a relationship with, but on the other hand I wanted to push her as far away as I could, because deep down I still thought of myself as someone who had no good traits or attributes whatsoever.

I remember the coach coming to pick up Susie for her trip to Darwin. She was reading the letter, I remember seeing a tear in her eye, as I think she could see from the tenure of the letter what I was trying to say. I know it was unfair of me to do this to her, but I guess I wanted her to know what sort of person I had become.

She did say at one stage that she was not going to go, but I insisted, and said it would give her time to make up her mind as to whether there was a long-term future for the both of us.

That evening, and once again this sounds strange, I was happy she had gone. By the very action she had gone, even though I had pushed her into going, it proved to me once again that I was not worthy of being loved. It had vindicated me completely, and I once again wallowed in the fact that no one could possibly love someone as useless as me.

The very next morning myself and Jo took the bus into town, this we would do every other day as this would enable us to get our food shopping and relax in Cairns city itself. It just so happened on this day that one of the residents of the retreat, a young Aussie, who I really didn't like anyway, relished in the fact that he could tell me he had seen Susie in town last night, they had partaken of a drink and one thing had led to another.

It was nothing major, apparently it was just a quick peck on the cheek, maybe slightly more, but to me my world at that time imploded. How could Susie do this to me? After all I had said to her, told her, how could she do this to me?

I don't know what I truly felt, all I knew was that yet again it had proven to me that I was not good enough for anyone to love, and it just backed up every argument I had in my head. I talked to Jo about this and she was lost for words. All she could say was that maybe a little too much alcohol had been consumed, and maybe Susie was 'confused'.

But, in my mind I had yet again been let down on a massive scale. There was no getting away from the fact that Susie had let me down so massively and wholeheartedly that I truly did not know which way to turn.

With this in mind, you would have thought that my next action would have been simple in the extreme. And I guess, if I had been thinking rationally and logically my next course of action would have made commonsense. But what you must remember is the fact that at this time in my life I truly was not thinking right, and for all intents and purposes, I did doubt my own sanity at times.

Susies trip was to take approximately four days. However, on the second night that Susie was in Darwin I received a phone call from her saying that she had fallen down some stairs at her hotel and twisted her ankle very badly. She was therefore going to get an early coach back to Cairns as she could in no way do the two trips that had been pre-booked, Kakadu and the surrounding areas.

It goes without saying that the atmosphere was somewhat tense when I met Susie from the coach. I had after all, told her about what I had heard. However, she was adamant that she did not wish to talk about it, but me being me, decided that this had to be thrashed out.

She explained to me that after having read the letter that I had written she was emotionally confused and very upset. She knew my history, and indeed she was very, very confused at the time. She told me that yes, she had drunk a lot of alcohol, and the gentleman concerned did push himself upon her to a degree, and all it was amounted to was no more than a quick snog.

But to me, it was far more than that. It had broken my trust utterly and completely, and I truly did not know which way to turn. Over a number of days we talked and talked, and tried to come to a conclusion.

Many of you will be saying that I was a fool, and extremely naïve when I said to Susie that I think we can go forward, and hopefully get over this hurdle in our new relationship. But to be honest, my mindset at the time was not at all logical. All I knew was that I had found someone who was prepared to love me, and show me that I was a worthy human being once again.

I do not regret my decision, whatsoever, but maybe at the time I admit, that the course of action I took may have been different if I had been thinking logically. However, what followed over the next seven years was truly a time of my life that I would never have experienced if it had not been for Susie. And for this I am truly thankful.

Confusion
****

As I said, Susie was on a working holiday and this necessitated the need that at times she would have to find alternative employment with different employers. A working holiday visa at that time dictated that she was only allowed to work for one employer for no more than three months at any one time.

It was decided for this reason that we would travel around Australia finding work as and when we could. Susie was very skilled in all office related matters, and indeed we thought she would be able to work wherever we found ourselves.

We truly had no long-term plan as to where and when we would go. But we knew deep down that this was going to be the adventure of a lifetime, and one that we both looked forward to immensely.

We decided that the best way of travelling around would be to relocate camper vans on behalf of rental companies. Basically, this involved phoning the local camper van rental companies and asking if they needed any of their vans relocating to a different part of Australia.

At times when a van hasn't been rented for a while one of the companies affiliates in another state or town will need a camper van due to the amount of bookings. This is when they 'employ' people to basically drive the camper van to a specific location at a specific time, and a specific date.

So in essence, we would phone the Cairns office of a camper van rental company and enquire as to whether they needed a van relocating anywhere in Australia. More often than not our enquiry led us to relocate a particular van from one state to another.

Our first journey was a relocation from Cairns to Sydney. They gave us approximately ten days to relocate their van and this would give us the opportunity to see a lot more of Australia. We picked the van up in Cairns and drove down the east coast stopping overnight anywhere that seemed a nice place to see.

However, even though the rental companies did give you a nominal amount for fuel, they didn't pay you as such, their main concern was the relocation of their vans to a specific point in time for the next order. So in reality, we were never going to make a lot of money travelling around Australia doing this.

Without boring you with the details we took some three months to travel around Australia and it was the adventure of a lifetime. We eventually ended up in Perth, and we decided to try and make a base for ourselves.

As I have said, I had previously been in Perth when my fathers work took him out there, and indeed myself and Jennie had experienced Perth. Whilst we were both enjoying our time immensely, work inevitably reared its ugly head. Susie did not take long to find work, after all, she was well versed and skilled in all aspects of clerical work, indeed, she was an asset to any company that would employ.

In the meantime I had to find suitable employment. I signed on with a local recruitment agency, and within a week was employed with one of the council's in Perth itself.

My work involved the maintenance and care of Canning City. As with most of us when we start a new job we are fairly tentative until we get to know people around us, all I can say about this new job is this.

That I have never met a more generous and well meaning group of workmates in all my life. My working day was full of laughter and friendly banter, and we always worked to our deadlines, there was not one day that we did not complete our work.

However, I guess you could say that at some stage I was living in cloud cuckoo land. No matter how hard I tried, the emotions I felt about my 'family' did have a huge impact on our new lives.

I do not know how at times Susie put up with me. She was indeed a saint, at times I pushed her to the limit, and if she ever gets to read this I can never put into words how much I appreciate what she did for me.

It would be very easy as a reader of this book to think that my life was now back on the straight and narrow, nothing could be further from the truth. There was not a day that went by that I did not think about my children back in the UK. But, what I had managed to do was simply this.

Mentally, I had managed to somehow put a brick wall up between the emotions I was feeling about my children and myself. At times this brick wall would crumble, and it was all I could do to carry on living. At these times I took my anger and frustration out on Susie. There were times when I was cruel, vindictive, and positively just plain difficult to live with.

Susie would occasionally walk in from work and she would be met with a face of thunder, and a deep depression. My usual comment would be 'You have no idea what it feels like to have two children taken off you'. And not once, not once, did Susie ever say to me that I was wrong.

She would soak up my abuse and my cruel remarks like a sponge, and eventually she would be able to calm me down. Not once did she retaliate and make the situation worse.

We were at this time living in a suburb of Perth called Subiaco, we had rented a small one bedroom flat which was our home for the next six months.

When I was in one of my black moods, and believe me, there were many, I took everything out Susie. I must have told her to leave me on no less than a dozen occasions, and indeed I packed her bags for her on many an occasion.

I would scream at her to leave me, and leave me alone and get on with her life. There were two main reasons for this. One, I was not at all convinced that I was worthy of Susies love, and secondly, I was convinced that one day she would leave me anyway, and that was a situation that I could not cope with.

On one occasion I remember packing her backpack for her and asking her to leave, or rather insisting that she left. With tears in her eyes, and after much confusion and shouting she walked out of the door and made her way down to the local train station.

I remember within five minutes of her leaving how lonely and heartbreakingly empty I felt. I have never felt such a sense of panic in all my life. I was alone again, everything had gone away from me, and it was my fault.

There was at this time a very popular song in the charts entitled 'When You're Gone', and as God is my witness this is the very next song that was played on the radio when Susie had walked out of the front door. The feelings and emotions I had at this time are indescribable, alone, vulnerable, and totally dissolute.

At this point I got in the car and drove as fast as I could to the station that I knew Susie was going to. I found her sitting on the platform looking forlorn and sad. No words that I said would ever be able to forgive my actions, it was all I could do to pluck up the courage to even meet her eye.

However, Susie being the lady she was embraced me and said very little, except for a few words of comfort and forgiveness.

As I've said, to this day I'm truly grateful to her for what she did for me, her patience, love, understanding and support at that time was what I needed, and indeed craved.

As time went by it was decided by the both of us that we would travel up to the north west of Australia, to see more of this great land. We had by this time enough money saved that enabled myself and Susie to buy a reliable car for the long journey up north.

We both agreed that while we wanted to get to Broome, we would stop off as much as we could so that we could see as much of Australia as possible. We decided that the best course of action would be to stop off in Carnarvon, and see if we could find employment.

This we did, and it was an experience that in no small measure both delighted me, and was one of the most horrific times of my life.

We were told before we arrived in Carnarvon that work and accommodation was going to be very difficult to find and source, however myself and Susie were never of the disposition of giving up, so we took the bull by the horns and travelled to Carnarvon.

It didn't take us long to source accommodation, a small family run unit that was run by a gentleman by the name of Sid. A friendly chap who it transpired would do all he could to help us find work.

I am not afraid of hard work, but the work myself and Susie were about to undertake was some of the hardest work I have ever done. We were basically employed as pepper pickers. This would involve picking peppers, red, green and yellow, from where they grew, which just happened to be on bush's that were around two foot tall.

The work was indeed backbreaking, bearing in mind that the temperatures at this time of year were in the early to mid 30's, I hope you can appreciate just how hard this work was. We would start work at approximately 7:30 a.m and finish around 5 p.m that afternoon.

It was indeed some of the hardest work we had ever done. Our backs, and legs ached beyond imagination, and it was all we could do to get ourselves back into the car for the twenty minute drive back to our unit. Once in the unit, we would collapse and stay seated for as long as we could, or rather when our muscles decided to once again relax a little and we could once again move.

The only way of making our bodies feel any better would have been to take the hottest of baths we possibly could, unfortunately, there was no such luxury as a bath, so a very hot shower had to suffice.

After several hours we would feel somewhat human yet again, eat, drink, and collapse into bed, knowing full well what the next day held in store for us.

After approximately two weeks in Carnarvon I made the normal phone calls that I made to home. I would as always try to speak to Jennie and the children, but this was always to no avail. I would also speak to my parents and let them know how we were getting on.

My parents always did their very best to sound as happy as they possibly could, but it was obvious that they were always worried about me. However, this one weekend was to be totally different.

I spoke to my dad first who told me everything was OK and he asked me about our plans. As always we had no plans set in concrete, but I tried to give my parents the barest outline of what we planned to do.

Then I spoke to my mum, it was obvious that there was something on her mind, I did all I could, without being rude to get it out of her.

It transpired, after long and protracted conversation that Jennie had been admitted to a local psychiatric unit. The impact this had me was immense, and it was one of the worst moments of my life.

After a further two or three minutes my mum told me that Jennie had been in the hospital for around two weeks, at this stage I was virtually hysterical with shock, and to some extent I took my feelings out on my parents. I asked my mum why on earth she hadn't told me before? All she could say was that she did not want me worrying on the other side of the world.

Looking back at that time I realised that my mum and dad were just trying to protect me, but at that time all I saw was my parents keeping news from me that I should have known about. Of course, whilst I was very concerned about Jennie, I was more concerned about my two children, and what was happening to them.

As you would imagine, from Australia at the best of times to talk to people can be extremely frustrating and difficult, bearing this in mind I hope you can imagine the trouble and problems that lay ahead trying to phone the psychiatric hospital Jennie had been admitted to.

I finally got through to the hospital and I explained to them who I was, while they were reticent to give me too much information as they only had my word that I was Jennies ex-husband I did eventually convince them of the facts and I asked them if I could speak to Jennie.

Obviously, after some debate, I was put through to Jennies ward. There were tears on both sides and she explained to me that the whole situation had got too much for her and it was recommended by her medical team that she should be admitted to to the hospital for analysis, but more importantly, to be looked after.

The conversation between myself and Jennie was the longest conversation we had had since we had split, unfortunately it was under the worst possible circumstances you could imagine.

I was phoning from a telephone box in the port area of Carnarvon which was extremely isolated. Susie always accompanied me to make these phone calls as she would speak to my parents, and her parents also. She could see that I was getting extremely upset, and she came over to try and comfort me.

I was nearly 10,000 miles away from a situation that I had little control over, and to be told that your ex-wife was in a psychiatric hospital was indeed a massive shock.

I eventually found out that my two children were staying with a relative of Jennies, whom had at the best of times had never really accepted me as Jennies husband. I tried to make several phone calls to these relatives, but was told in no uncertain terms that it had nothing to do with me and I should stay away.

I remember coming off the telephone and my first words to Susie were, 'I have got to go back and sort the situation out'. Susie as ever was supportive and loving, and she showed me that she would stand by my side no matter what. The drive back to the unit seemed to take an eternity, all I wanted to do was to arrange a plane flight home, and in someway try to sort this mess out.

I contacted Nigel my solicitor and explained the situation to him. I asked him to contact Jennies family and tell them I was going to come back to take care of my two children. I hoped in someway that this would be possible, as even the hardest of souls would see how concerned I was, and would do all they could to help me.

I rang Nigel the very next day and asked him if he had managed to contact the family, he said he had, but unfortunately they were going to do all they could to ensure that I was not allowed to see my children. I have no idea how to this day I remained sane, and to some degree logical. I could not believe that this was the situation.

I was frantically trying to see my children and make sure that they were OK, but this was to be to no avail. I knew from past history that I would never be allowed to see my two children, even under these circumstances.

I can forgive a lot, but this, I have never been able to forgive, and I will never forgive. Nigel made all of the applications to court about me having access to the children, but yet again the relatives concerned did everything they could to put obstacles in my way, once again using the so-called evidence that I had punched Jane, and threatened Jennie.

There were frantic phone calls to my parents to try and find out a little bit more about the situation, each and every time my parents told me that they had done all they could to try and get me access to see my two children, but each and every time this had been to no avail.

I was totally and utterly devastated, my mind, the sane part at least, told me that I had to go back to the UK, but after yet another phone call with Nigel it was made obvious that this was going to be extremely difficult. Nigel told me that if I did go back to the UK there was legislation in place that would involve the police and social services stopping me having access to my children.

To try and convey to you just how I felt is nearly impossible, I was sad, tremendously upset, confused and utterly bereft at the thought of not being able to see my two children, and also not being able to help Jennie. Even though things hadn't gone well between myself and Jennie I was still concerned very much for her welfare, and wanted to make sure that she was OK.

I blamed myself totally and utterly for the situation that was unfolding before my eyes, and no matter who tried to tell me it was not my fault I could not see this. All I knew was this, that my ex-wife was now in a psychiatric hospital, my two children were now living with someone who cared little for anyone but themselves, and basically they could not care less what happened to me.

By this time because of my mindset I wasn't a particularly nice person to live with. Susie was the obvious target of my frustration, and for several days I treated her appallingly. Once again, I asked her to leave and I would sort this mess out, I told her that I was not worthy of any one loving me, or indeed looking after me, and I just wanted her to go away.

However, she never once walked out of the door, or indeed lost her temper with me. She was at that time my rock, support, and loving partner. She never rose to anything I said, in actual fact she sat there and took it, and not once did she offer an opinion except for sympathy, love and understanding.

Susie was indeed one in a million, and she showed me a side of human nature that I thought was in short supply at this particular time. We sat and talked for hours and hours about what I should do. The obvious thing to do would have been to travel back to the UK and try and sort this mess out, but control had been utterly taken away from me, and little I said, or did would have any impact on the situation.

I truly had no idea about why Jennie was in hospital, she had told me the barest of outlines, that the whole situation had got too much for her and she felt as if she had indeed experienced a mental breakdown. I knew little of the actual situation, only at a much later date would the true horror come to light.

Myself and Susie made phone calls every day back to the UK to check on the situation, but each and every time we were told that it had nothing to do with us, and we were not to keep calling.

I rang social services, the hospitals, Jennies doctors, but was told that I had no right to know any more information, as certain members of Jennies family had put into place mandates that basically excluded me from knowing anything.

I cannot put into words what sort of mindset I was in at this time, all I know is that I thought I was going mental with frustration and worry, and to be kept being told that I had no right to even speak with my children just exasperated the whole situation.

A lot of you at this stage will be asking yourself one question. And it is this. Why didn't I just get on the next plane home and try to sort the situation out? I would of said the same thing many years ago, but until you are in this kind of situation it is a difficult thing to try and explain.

I admit, that all I wanted to do was get back to the UK and try my very best to sort the situation out. But I knew in my heart of hearts that by me going back to the UK this would impact on my children. I knew only too well that I would never be allowed to see my children, and the arguments and legalities of trying to do so would only impact on my children immensely.

I wanted to at all times, protect my children from what was going on, this includes the separation of myself and Jennie, and the ongoing situation we found ourselves in. It is only now that I can look back at these times and realise my actions were true and correct.

Many of you will say that I was a coward not to go back to the UK, but please bear in mind that all I wanted to do was to protect my children and shield them from any of the arguments that would have taken place. At no point in time did I want the children hurt or put through any more stress than they were already under, so a decision was made to stay in Australia and try our best to monitor it from there.

Rightly or wrongly, it was a decision based on emotion and fact. There were certain members of Jennies family that would do all they could to destroy me, and wipe any impact I had on my children's lives away.

By this time myself Susie were not only exhausted, but also emotionally drained. We thought the situation could not get any worse, but yet again we were to be surprised.

A further two weeks went past and I received a letter from Jennie. It basically said that she was out of hospital and back with my two children. However, it did say one other thing, and it was simply this.

Jennie had met someone else and she was now applying officially for a divorce. She had not told me how long she had known this person, or indeed where she had met him. And I guess, it was none of my business, as we had both separated and we both had a right to get on with our lives.

But the letter was still a shock, as far as I knew Jennie had still been in hospital and my two children with relatives. Now I was told that she had the children back, a new man in her life, and wanted a divorce as soon as possible.

What happened next was a decision that I regret wholeheartedly. I only regret it because I can look back at this time and realise that maybe I should have done things differently.

The divorce papers that were sent to me by Jennies solicitor basically said that I had been the one at fault for the separation due to my behaviour toward Jennie and my children, I think the exact wording used was 'unreasonable behaviour'.

If I had been thinking correctly my next course of action may have been different. But from previous experience, and a sense of misguided guilt I decided to sign the paperwork without any arguments. There was one other reason why I decided not to offer any resistance. I thought, however wrongly, that if I went along with what had been said then surely my family could once again be happy and contented.

Jennies stay in hospital was now a distant memory. I thought that by signing the paperwork and admitting to any blame apportioned to me that at the very least Jennie would once again be able to live a life that was happier, without me around.

Susie did however say to me that I cannot possibly sign it as it will, or could be held against me in the future. She was adamant in the fact that I should not accept the blame for the divorce on these grounds. Looking back at this time, I guess she was right, but there was only one thought in my mind at that time.

All I wanted was for Jennie to be happy, and if this was a possibility then it would ultimately make my children happy also. If she had found a new man and they were living in a stable environment this meant that my children would now be able to carry on with their lives, happy, contented and fulfilled.

I won't go into any great detail of what was said in the divorce papers, suffice to say that for all intents and purposes I was being portrayed as a monster, a bad husband, and awful father. All I wanted was for Jennie and the children to be happy, if this meant that I took the blame for the marriage breakdown then so be it. I would not listen to what Susie told me, I signed the paperwork and sent it off the very next afternoon.

Susie had made her feelings very obvious, but after I had sent the paperwork back she did not say another word on the matter. That's the sort of person she was, she would offer an opinion, but at the end of the day she would support what I had done.

By this time the pepper picking season was coming to an end, and it was obvious that we would have to at some point either stay in Carnarvon and find other work, or we would have to travel to a different part of Australia and hopefully find gainful employment.

We took the decision to travel to Broome to try and find accommodation and work once again. Within two days of making this decision we arrived in Broome, and immediately set about trying to source accommodation and jobs.

As ever, we were told that we would never find it easy in Broome, as it was the height of the tourist season and all accommodation was full, and jobs the were taken. However, within three days I had found employment on a full-time basis working in a service station. We had also found accommodation in a holiday park in a tiny one bedroomed unit. Though not perfect, this suited us fine, and we soon got used to the confined area.

Susie found work within a further two weeks working as a waitress in one of the many restaurants in Broome. It was the peak tourist season so we were both very busy and rushed off our feet.

I worked six days a week, from six in the morning till three in the afternoon. Whilst these were very early mornings it did give me the opportunity to have the afternoons free and still pursue my love of fishing.

Myself and Susie were by this time once again drinking excessively, though this drinking did not impact on either of our jobs, we could still see that we were drinking far too much.

We would often by a litre of Jack Daniel's, and several boxes of wine, and these would be consumed within two or three days. Most evenings would see us drink to excess, but we still managed to run our daily lives in a relatively organised manner.

As you can imagine, the situation with my children and Jennie still played a hugely significant part in our lives. There wasn't a minute that went past that I did not think about my children and how I can best serve them. The feelings of homesickness and worry were immense, and at times it was all I could do to stop myself getting on the next plane back to the UK.

After some six months in Broome myself and Susie decided that we should take a trip back to the UK to see what we could do. Though I doubted there was anything we could do, the instinct to run and see my children was immense.

We arrived back in the UK on a cold October morning and once again stayed with my parents for a number of weeks until we got settled in.

By this time I was full of trepidation as to how best go about talking to Jennie and seeing my children once again. I had by this time managed to speak to Jennie on several occasions about seeing her and the children on our return, and it was agreed that initially my parents would pick up my children from Jennies house and bring them back to their house so I could see them.

Susie was with me at this time and to say she was worried sick would be an understatement. I don't know who was more nervous, Susie or me. My children were not told that I was going to be there at the time, as I thought it best for all concerned if they did not know. I did not want them to get too worked up or excited at the thought of seeing me again.

But if I was totally honest I thought that they may have been told certain things about me that would make them hate me. At the very least I thought that if they did not know I was awaiting their arrival I would be able to see them before they ran away from me because of what they had been told.

I remember I was sitting in my old bedroom waiting for the door to open. My parents and children arrived at around 10:30 a.m and I remember thinking, do I run or do I face them? After all, I had no idea what they had been told about me. They might have been frightened of me, scared, or even terrified of seeing such a terrible dad once again.

Jane was the first to come into the bedroom and see me, her face was a picture, firstly it went blank, then wide eyed, then a massive grin came across her face and she screamed for Betty to come and see what was in the bedroom.

They both stood there as if nothing had happened, children have the ability to bounce back a lot quicker than adults and the welcome I got off my kids was a memory that has never gone away from me. They hugged me, kissed me, and one question came from their lips. 'Dad, are you staying'?

I cannot possibly put into words just what thoughts and emotions went through my mind at this time. Firstly, to see my children after so many months away was something that I will never be able to explain to anyone. But more importantly, was the fact that my children had asked me this one question.

They were basically saying that they wanted me to stay and be part of their lives. Once again, I find it nearly impossible to explain to you as a reader how this made me feel. In a perfect world everything would have been fine, and indeed my long-term future would have been sorted from this moment in time. But this is far from a perfect world, and to think otherwise is foolhardy.

The Warmth Of Children
****

The rest of the day was full of laughter and chit chat, it was difficult to try and explain to my children exactly what had gone on. They only saw that their 'dad' was back and all was fine and dandy.

But the adults involved knew that this was going to be a very difficult situation to try and rectify. To try and explain to children of that age the mistakes, sadness, and absolute misery that is involved in a marriage breakdown is not only impossible, but also, very unfair in the extreme.

Once my children were dropped off in the evening by my parents we were all absolutely exhausted. Susie as ever had been my rock and we both sat down and talked about what we were going to do in the future. I don't think either of us really knew what was about to unfold, but for once we were talking about the positives of our future lives.

Though the majority of communication between myself and Jennie was done through my parents I did at times have the opportunity to speak with her. But, even though I wanted to know exactly what had gone on I thought it not my place to ask too much. She seemed to be in a far better place than she was many months ago. I thought that if I pushed this point too far it might upset her and that is the last thing I wanted to do.

Even though we were officially divorced, I had no intention whatsoever of upsetting her, as I just wanted to see her, my children and her new husband live a life that was full of happiness without me making it anymore difficult.

It was agreed between myself and Jennie that I would be able to see my children every two weeks, though realistically this was never going to be enough, I thought it best if I went along with this as it seemed to keep everyone, except myself, happy.

Things went along fairly smoothly for all while. We would get to see my children every other weekend and we would all go out for the day, or just make the most of a wet weekend. Our days were full of happiness and laughter, and it was indeed a joy that we were together again.

However, there was one aspect of this relationship that was never going to go away. I knew only too well that my children, Jennie and her new husband had new lives and I was only a very small part of it. It was always made obvious to me that while I may have been the children's father, I was to have no influence of any great significance in their future upbringing.

I also knew only too well that the present situation I found myself in, the so called 'happy' atmosphere, would only last for a certain period of time due to other peoples influence.

It wasn't long before their influence impacted on my life once again. After only several months, phone calls were often made the day before I was due to see my children and our weekends with them were cancelled.

Many reasons were given for this, the children had colds, they had parties to go to, or they were far too tired. Each and every reason I understood, and not once did I ever kick up a fuss. Even though at times I knew only too well that the reasons given were untrue.

I knew that if I did make a fuss then it would only take a phone call from certain member of the family to stop me having access completely. A lot of what went on no one else was witness to. I am not prepared to go into any greater detail within this book about what was said to me, and indeed done to me over the next few months. Out of respect, however misguided, I am not prepared to do such a thing.

No one knows to this day the lengths certain parties went to in order to try and destroy me, and in no small measure they nearly succeeded. There were certain people around at that time that made my life a living hell, and it was obvious that they wanted my relationship with my children to fail all costs, and they would do all they could facilitate this.

As I've said, I am not prepared to go into any great detail, you will see the reasons later why I have chosen to take this path.

Suffice to say, that I knew that one day in the not too distant future my relationship with the children would once again be put under immense stress and pressure.

However, I could see, or rather thought I could see that Jennie was now once again in a happy relationship, and she was for all intents and purposes a lot better now that she had a stable home environment.

It was at this point in time that myself and Susie had to sit down and talk about our future. Any future I had, I always knew would involve Australia. Yes, I had two children in the UK that I loved dearly and would do anything for, but they were now in an environment that they seemed happy and contented, and if the truth were known, even though I had my children around me, to some degree, when it was deemed fit by others, I still knew that Australia was going to play a huge part not only in my life, but all those that knew me.

By this time, myself and Susie were trying to sort out our future careers. Susie was fortunate in the fact, no, not fortunate, she had worked extremely hard, that she was in a position of being able to find work relatively quickly and this she did at one of the biggest employers within Essex. She enjoyed her job immensely, though at times, as we all do, she had her bad days.

I on the other hand, was a different story. I was never very career orientated, but would always be able to find work when I had to. But, there was one big difference. In order for me to look after my children, it was obvious that I would have to find employment that had much more of a long-term future.

Bearing this in mind, I decided that I would become a driving instructor. I had always enjoyed driving, and would often take myself off in the middle of the night and just drive where ever I fancied. I thought as I enjoyed driving there would be no reason why I would not enjoy teaching people to drive.

I enrolled with a local driving school and started my driving and instructional training a few brief weeks later. It was indeed a very comprehensive and difficult skill to learn. The training involved was immense, and at times very, very taxing. After all, to be able to teach someone to drive takes great skill, patience and practice.

If I were successful with my training then I would become a franchised driving instructor with the local driving school I was training with. I was fortunate in that I passed all of my exams first time, and was granted an ADI registration to start my teaching career.

The job was often very intense and at times the stress levels involved were huge, but for the most part I did enjoy my time teaching people to drive, there were however a few times I nearly reached for the valium, but all in all, I enjoyed it immensely.

The relationship by this time between myself and children was going along very well, however, there was always a constant threat from a certain member of Jennies family that this would be taken away at any point in time.

I could have fought back, but in the interests of everyones sanity, not least my children, not wanting to see them upset in any way, I decided to bite my tongue, keep my head down, and just get on with it.

Within several months the pressure put upon myself was immense by certain people. I never once cracked, or gave into the temptation to fight back, I knew only too well that this would have a detrimental impact on all those involved.

Susie, being the person that she was, had always said that she wanted to make a home in Australia, but, she also realised that I had two children back in UK, and they had to be our main concern. Whilst I agreed that Australia was indeed an ideal location for us to build a future, I did have to take into consideration my two children, and Jennie to a lesser extent.

The relationship between myself and Jennie whilst not being perfect, was communicative. Or rather, communicative on my behalf. I would have willingly gone round and seen Jennie with no problem at all, and exchanged polite conversation with her. I had no particular axe to grind with her, what had gone on in the past had happened, and there was little we could do about this.

I was not about to drag up the past about what she had said about me, why she was in hospital, and how she had let the children down. To have brought such subjects up would have not only upset all those involved, but would have changed nothing.

By this time myself and Susie had talked incessantly about going back to Australia. My relationship with my children now was one of honesty and openness. They had gained their trust in me once again and realised that Australia did mean an awful lot to me.

Myself and Susie had explained to them that one day we would return to Australia to live, but only when it was appropriate to do so would we do such a thing. After all, they were still very young and had little realisation of what had taken place in the past, and what might take place in the future.

I was not about to tell them of what went on between myself and certain members of the family, in their eyes the person in question was one that they loved and respected, and I was not about to try and influence their opinion in anyway. I just wish the person in question had shown me the same courtesy I was showing them.

Eventually, myself and Jennie did talk openly and honestly, and we could be fairly frank about our future. I could see, or rather thought I saw that she was happy and contented in her new marriage. She could also see that I missed Australia with all my heart, and this was talked about often.

We agreed that if we ever went back to Australia, now that Jennie was in a better mindset she would be able to explain to the children just exactly what was taking place. It was also agreed that a certain person's influence, even though I hadn't even told Jennie what had gone on, would be negated to a certain extent, and Jennie would make it clear to them that she, and she alone would tell the children, and she would explain to the children what was happening.

I was under the impression that Jennie and her new husband were perfectly happy, and for all intense and purposes all was OK. Of course there were times when the situation was fraught, but this is the norm in most marriages, so why should this be any different?

I now had access to my children every other weekend, well nearly, and it now seemed as though we were all in a routine. Susie was enjoying her job immensely, and my driving career was progressing fairly well.

All those involved knew that one day myself and Susie would return to Australia, but for the time being we all settled into somewhat, mundane lives.

We were now living in a very rural setting and this was indeed great comfort to us as we could often take long walks with the children to blow the cobwebs away.

As I said, life was now being lived on a far more level plain, and was to the outsider, a life that was complete in every way. However, things were about to change drastically for all those involved.

Absolute Desolation
****

In September of 2006 myself and Susie decided that we would buy ourselves a dog. After all, we were very keen dog lovers, and where we now lived would give us the opportunity to give our new dog plenty of walks and exercise. My job as a driving instructor gave me the opportunity to pop home throughout the day to make sure the dog was alright.

We went down many avenues to purchase a dog. The RSPCA, etc, but at times we could not find a dog that was suitable for our needs. I was trawling through the internet as I always did before any decision was made, and I happened across a site that even surprised me.

There was a breed of dog that was called an 'Australian Shepherd', I didn't even know such a breed was in existence. But after prolonged and protracted thought, myself and Susie decided that we would do all we could to buy one of these dogs, after of course, a lot of research and deliberation.

We were fortunate enough that there was a breeder about a two hours drive from us, so I duly contacted this breeder to see if they could tell us more.

Within a few hours arrangements were put into place, and I was to take a trip to Suffolk to discuss further what was entailed in owning such a dog. The breeder was a terrific lady and spoke at great length about the positives and negatives of such a breed, and what was needed from us.

Of course our main concern was that the dog had to be good with children, was sociable and easily trained. Whilst this was found to be the case, I of course told the breeder that I would discuss our prospective purchase with Susie first. I had been able to see the new puppy at great length, but because of Susies work commitments she had been unable to attend on this first occasion.

So arrangements were made that the next weekend myself and Susie would once again travel to Suffolk so that we could both speak with the breeder, and the breeder in turn could interview, (vet) us to make sure we were the type of people that could look after an Australian Shepherd.

As is the case with purchasing a dog we made the house ready, things that could be chewed, eaten or destroyed were put away, or moved out of reach, and the house was ready for our new arrival.

Two weeks after our initial enquiry to the breeder we travelled to Suffolk to pick up our new puppy. We arrived on a rain soaked day in September, excited and overjoyed at what lay ahead of us.

Papers were signed, food stored, and myself, Susie and 'Knox' piled into the car for the journey home. As you would imagine the journey home was rather tense and fraught. The new pup insisted on trying to claw and chew itself out of the puppy carrier we had taken with us.

On more than a dozen occasions we pulled over to the side of the road and made sure our new pup was OK and not getting too stressed by his new environment. It was on one such occasion about halfway through our journey when my mobile phone rang. Many of my pupils would ring me changing times or dates of their lessons, but this was different.

The number that came up was not recognised, seeing as some of my pupils would often ring from an unrecognised number I decided to answer it anyway.

The conversation that followed was one that I shall remember till my dying, it still sends a shiver down my spine.

The lady on the other end of the phone was from a national mental health unit and she introduced herself as Maria. After some very long and protracted conversations relating to me proving who I was, she informed me that something had occurred at my children's house, and I was asked to get there as soon as possible.

She would say no more than that. All she requested was that I travel to my children's address, and come as soon as possible. Bearing in mind that myself and Susie had just picked up our new addition we were at a loss as to what to say or do.

After the initial panic we decided that I would drop off Susie and pup, and then I would travel over to the children's house and find out was the hell was going on.

It was at the very best an hours drive from our house to my children's, but this was indeed going to be one of the longest drives of my life. I said goodbye to Susie at the front door and made my way to Jennies house.

Unless you have ever been in this position it is very difficult to put into words exactly what was going thorough my mind. The nurse had told me at the initial conversation that even though the situation was rather fraught, my children were fine and no harm had come to them. This was one saving grace, but it still did beg the question as to what had actually occurred?

The journey seemed to take an eternity, it just never seemed to end. I am not normally one for breaking the law, but on this occasion I must of broken every speed limit there was.

I eventually arrived at my children's address and what lay before me was a nightmare of massive proportions. An ambulance, police car and several other vehicles were parked outside Jennies house.

Within thirty seconds of arriving I saw Jennie come out of the front door screaming and yelling at the top of her voice. All she kept saying was 'Sorry' to me. I had no idea at all of what was going on. I was at a loss as to what to do or say.

Jennie was dressed in little else except for a dressing gown and slippers. She was running around screaming at the top of her voice. There were several people around, including ambulance staff who tried to calm her, but she would hear little of it.

By this time I had managed to catch hold of Jennie and calm her down ever so slightly. She was sobbing and just kept saying that she was 'Sorry'. I had no real idea of why she was apologising to me, except maybe for the fact that this situation had arisen.

By this time I had managed to calm Jennie down

significantly, also a lady from social services had taken control and fortunately managed to calm the situation a little more.

Before I had a chance to say or do anything else Jennie was led into an ambulance and it drove away from the rather tense situation. It was at this point that my two children came out of the house, bemused, shocked and looking extremely frightened.

They were as white as a sheet and very nearly dumb struck. I went over to them and asked them what on earth had gone on? Bearing in mind that I didn't want to ask them too much, I thought it best if I kept my questions to a minimum.

All they said to me was that their new stepfather had gone out screaming and shouting, they had no idea where he was, and apparently Jennie had reacted as I had just seen. That is all I knew, nothing more or nothing less. I was what you could call, tremendously confused.

As I got the children into my car and tried my best to reassure them, I saw in their faces absolute fear and trepidation. It was at this point in time that a gentleman from social services came over to me to have a chat.

His words to some degree fell upon stony ground. I had just seen my ex-wife taken away in an ambulance, and my two children scared out of their wits. Whatever he said to me was going to miss its mark somewhat. I needn't have worried though. The conversation was brief and to the point.

All he said to me was that there had been a situation at Jennies house, and would I be kind enough to look after my children for that night and someone would contact me the next day. I didn't want to increase the stress all around at this stage, so I did as he said and got my two children out of the situation as quickly as possible, without asking any more questions.

The drive home was filled with an atmosphere that you could virtually cut with a knife. The conversation between myself and the children was staid, I refused to ask them too much as I didn't want them to get upset.

We arrived home tired, exhausted and utterly shattered. As

I knocked at the door I truly had no idea what had just happened, or indeed what the future held. We all went in doors and myself and Susie did our best to reassure the children that everything would be OK. I doubt they believed us, but nonetheless, we both tried our very best to do what we could for them.

Susie as ever was marvellous. Tea was cooked, beds were made and the children settled down and put to bed. I doubt that they got much sleep that night, I know myself and Susie spent most of the night awake trying to figure out what the hell had just gone on.

Bearing in mind that this night was unlike any other. We had just picked up our new dog and now we had my children in the same house. The dog spent most of the night whining from downstairs and would insist on being a complete pain in the backside. This combined with the situation that had just unfolded, made for a night to remember.

Social Services. Madness
****

I took the next day off work and tried my best to make some sense of what had gone on. The children's schools were telephoned and told the barest outline of what had happened, and I explained to them that as soon as I hear any news I would of course let them know.

My next phone call was to social services. This was going to prove to be one of the most difficult conversations I had ever had. I understand only too well the need for privacy in such matters, but what transpired that day even surprised me.

The lady at the other end of the telephone would tell me little of what was going on. All I was told was that there had been a 'situation' at Jennies house, and would I be good enough to look after my children.

I was told no more than that. Except for this. That the situation at my children's house had become untenable, and Jennie had basically had a mental breakdown. That was all I was told. Nothing more.

At this point in time I was beginning to pull my hair out. I needed to know what had gone on, but all I was told was that if I wanted to know more I would have to be given permission by Jennie.

I could not believe what the hell was going on. No matter what I said, or did, I was not going to get anywhere. As far as social services were concerned I was their 'father', but I was not allowed to know any more.

I came off the phone utterly confused and to some degree hopping mad. I was at a loss as to what to do next. So I did the obvious thing and rang Susie. I told her of the situation and what had just occurred. She was as normal, calm and collected, and did her best to reassure me.

The next few days were a constant battle with the authorities. All I wanted to know was what had happened, what I needed to do next. But each and every time I tried to get some answers I was faced with the same response. I was not allowed to know anymore until Jennie gave her permission.

Jennie was of course in hospital once again. I was faced with a decision that was very difficult to address. Do I contact Jennie in hospital and ask her to explain what had gone on?

The only thought that went through my mind was that if I did take such a path would this exasperate the situation and make things a whole lot worse. I had no real idea of what I should do next. In the end I decided that I would go over to the children's house and see their stepfather, Steve.

I had spoken to him, and indeed seen him on many occasions, and for all intense and purpose he came over as a nice enough chap who I thought I could talk to.

I went over that evening and was welcomed by Steve. I did my best to be polite and gracious, but all I wanted to know was what the hell had gone on? Steve explained to me the barest of outlines. Apparently, Jennie was finding everything a little too much. She was very depressed and anxious, and had apparently had a nervous breakdown.

I could not understand why this had occurred. Each and every time I spoke to Jennie or the children in the past they all seemed OK, nothing untoward was ever highlighted.

I asked Steve once again why Jennie had got so depressed? He was fairly cagey with his response, but just said that things at home had become rather tense, and with the added worry of money concerns had taken their toll on the family as a whole.

I could not believe that this was the only reason. After all, the situation I had experienced was catastrophic in its impact and I thought that there had to be more to this situation than first met the eye. I was not going to be fobbed off with these reasons. I pushed and pushed Steve until he finally gave me a straight answer, or at least at that time I thought a straight answer. It transpired that Jennies mother had past away some ten days earlier, the impact that it had on the family was immense.

Jennie had lost her mum to a terrible disease, she had indeed been going thorough hell for the past three or four weeks. To lose a mum in these circumstances is beyond imagination unless you have lived through it.

I asked Steve why no one had told me. He said that they wanted to keep it as a private matter and they wanted to deal with their grief in their own way.

I understood this to some extent, but nonetheless if I had known about the situation I may have been able to help in some small way. I had no idea how I would of done this, but I was sincere in my offer.

The rest of the evening was spent with polite conversation and for all intense and purposes my mind was to some small extent, put at ease. We discussed what should happen with the children and which course of action we should take.

I was of course more than willing to look after my children for as long as it took. There was never a doubt in my mind that I would do all I could to help the situation. And besides, to have my children back with me for a while at least, was wonderful.

Because of my job as a driving instructor my hours were somewhat flexible. I could arrange lessens around the children and make sure that they were well looked after. The girl's schools were also only minutes from Susies workplace, so it was no trouble to drop them off at school, or indeed pick them up.

Myself and Steve discussed what should happen next and we both came to the conclusion that myself and Susie would take care of the children for the foreseeable future. Steve after all, had full-time employment, and his hours of work did in no small measure impact on his ability to look after the children by himself.

Maybe I was naïve in the extreme. But I thought Steve was being a very reasonable chap, and we both thought it best if myself and Susie look after the children as this would allow him to carry on working and making sure the family home was also looked after.

In my naivety I thought he had the best interests of Jennie and the children foremost in his mind, and of course I would do all I could to help the family out. It was only later that I was to discover his ulterior motives for the course of action he took.

By this time myself and Susie were doing all we could to ensure that the children were in a caring and loving home. We did all we could to ensure that they were happy, contented and fulfilled. However, this was against the backdrop of a situation that we had little control over.

Jennie was still in hospital, hopefully getting better by the day. I would often try and speak with her, and on one or two occasions did manage to hold a brief conversation with her.

Without putting undue pressure on her I would tentatively ask her why on earth she hadn't told me about the situation at home, and particularly her mums death? I explained to her that I would of done all I could to help, no matter how insignificant this help may have been, all she had to do was ask me, nothing would have been too much trouble.

Jennie would just say that she thought it best if the situation was kept within the family and not to worry me. I took this at face value, as I was at this time beginning to think that there was more to this situation than first met the eye. But I kept my thoughts to myself, and thought the best course of action would be to keep my views private.

By this time the children had become accustomed to how myself and Susie were trying to deal with the situation. They never offered an opinion on what had gone on, and I for one was not about to question this thought process. They after all, seemed fairly happy within themselves, bearing in mind the situation they found themselves in.

School runs, dropping them off at friends, were all just now a day to day occurrence. Susie was as ever, a rock, and did all she could to help the situation. Nothing was too much trouble for her and I count my blessings at this time that I had her as my support.

It was now the beginning of December. At this stage I had no communication with Jennies side of the family whatsoever. Not once did they ask to talk to me about what was going on. After all, they seemed to have all of the relevant information at their disposal. They knew far more than me, but at no time would I be informed about what was going on.

I guess from previous history I cannot blame them for this, but nonetheless I would of liked the briefest of updates concerning the situation. But at the end of the day my children's welfare was my main concern, and I thought that the lack of communication was best for all involved.

Social services would occasionally phone me up and ask how the children were, but that was all they ever said. No matter how many times I asked to be kept informed I was met by silence. I still had no idea what had truly gone on.

In the second week of December I was told by social services that Jennie had been released from hospital and was well on the road to recovery. I knew only too well the next action that was about to take place.

Deep in my heart I knew that one day soon the children would in all probability go back to Jennie. It was a day myself and Susie were dreading, we knew sooner or later that this situation would arise.

It came as no surprise that the following week social services did indeed contact us and ask that they come around to conduct an 'interview'. We had no real idea about what was entailed in such an interview, but were told the barest outline of what was going to happen.

The interview would be to determine what should happen to the children next. 'Determine' is a word that conjures up many different scenarios, none of which I found particularly savoury.

I knew Jennie had been released from hospital so I thought it best if I try and speak to her first. She was fairly communicative and forthcoming. She basically told me that she was now in a far better place. Yes, she had been a victim of a mental breakdown, but she assured me that she was back to her normal self.

She was also very apologetic that it had come to this situation, and that both myself and Susie had been put in this position. I explained to her that there was no need to apologise as these things happen.

But I did want assurances that she was now fully recovered and could cope once again. She told me that this was indeed the case and there would be no future issues to contend with. I took her at her word, but was insistent that if this sort of thing ever happened again, I had to know about it.

Jennie also explained to me that the reason the social services were coming around to our house was to evaluate the children's opinion on where they wanted to live in the future.

This filled me and Susie with dread, for one reason and one reason alone. Myself, Susie and the children had spoken often of what their future held. We had explained to them that at some point in the future their mum would be released from hospital and in all likely hood their mum would want them back.

They were both now old enough to realise that this was the case and indeed have an opinion on their future. When all is said and done the vast majority of the time children would rather be with their mums rather than their dads.

That sounds very harsh, but I will try and explain. No matter how good a dad is, no matter what he does for his children, no matter the sacrifices made, the vast majority of the time young children would rather be bought up by their mums, rather than their dads.

It is a fact of life, that at times can be a difficult pill to swallow. But when all is said and done the welfare of the children has to come first. And that welfare has to include their future happiness.

As I said, we had all discussed this often, and no matter how difficult to accept we had little doubt that the children would want to go back to their mum. At times these conversations were extremely difficult and upsetting. But all of the options had to be discussed, at great length.

In essence the question was simple. 'Kids, you know that your mum has had a difficult time. But she is know a lot better. She loves you both very much and can't wait to see you again. Be honest, where would you prefer to live in the future? With myself and Susie, or back with your mum and Steve? We need your honest opinion. No matter what you say we will go along with what you want. Myself and Susie both realise that you love us dearly, and to say that you want to live with your mum again may well make you feel very guilty. But we need to know exactly what you want. Of course we will miss you, we both love you very much, but at the end of the day your happiness is our main priority, and we need you to be honest'.

That is somewhere near the tenure of the many conversations that we had. Myself and Susie never put any pressure on them. We just needed them to know that their honest opinions would be met with understanding and concern.

All they would ever say was 'Mum, sorry'. This was said through tears and great sadness. They were old enough to realise that these few words meant everything. The feelings of guilt and heartbreak they had are indescribable. To see their faces with tears streaming down their cheeks sends a chill up my spine to this day.

But, it was obvious that they did indeed want to return to their mum and Steve, and I and Susie were not about to make them feel any worse. We had to except the fact that this was the children's wishes, and we had little choice in the matter.

We would of dearly loved have them live with us forever more, we would of moved heaven and earth to make this happen, if they had wanted this. But it was blatantly obvious that their hearts lay elsewhere, and it was decision that we all had to live with.

The day came when social services was due to come to our house. It was arranged that they would call in the evening when we were all settled and relaxed. Somehow the word 'relaxed' is somewhat inappropriate. Myself and Susie were a bundle of nerves, and it was all we could do to hold ourselves together for all of our sakes, let alone the children.

At precisely 7:30 p.m there came a knock at the door, for one brief moment we all looked at each other as if time had stood still. The children had been made aware that social services were going to call round that evening, and that they had to be completely honest with whoever showed up.

I opened the door and was greeted by a smiling, rather plump lady by the name of Helen. I asked her in and offered her a cup of tea in the hope that this would in someway break the ice and make the atmosphere slightly more relaxed.

Helen came over as a very nice, concerned, and honest individual. But, as the conversation progressed we were to find out that even though myself and Susie had taken care of the children for nearly three months we were still not informed of what was truly going on.

The children were sitting on the sofa, I dare say trying to assimilate what was being said. In their young minds they must have been totally confused, and a little worried. They knew at some point in time this lady from social services was going to ask them their opinion.

I had never experienced social services before, and hopefully I never do in the future, so with this in mind I hope you can understand how not only I felt, but Susie also.

I was full of questions that I wanted to ask, and in response, be answered. But this was not going to be the case at all. It was made blatantly obvious from the minute Helen walked into our house that she was there purely to see how the children were doing.

I can understand this completely, but it still dumbfounded me that I and Susies questions and opinions were in no small measure ignored, and for all intents and purposes completely cast aside.

All I wanted to know was that if the children did go back to Jennies house that they would be OK and their welfare would be looked after. My main concern was their long-term happiness, and their ability to become a family unit once more.

I wanted to be reassured that Jennie was indeed in a fit state, both physically and mentally so that she could look after the children in the way that any child should be looked after. I questioned Helen if this was indeed the case, and all she would say was that Jennie was now, at that time, in control of her life, and wanted the children back as soon as possible.

I asked Helen if there was anything else I should know about the situation at home, but was told in no uncertain terms that it was none of my business what had happened. I questioned Helen yet again, and said to her quite simply that what I was asking was being asked out of concern, worry, and stress for the long-term happiness of my children.

At no point in time would she tell me any more, all she would say was that Jennie and Steve were now in a position of being able to look after the children properly once again.

At times I became extremely frustrated, and in no small measure annoyed at the brick wall that was facing me. As a concerned and anxious dad I thought I would be entitled to know exactly what my children were going back to, but all Helen would say was that the children would be cared enough for in an appropriate manner, if indeed they wanted to return to their mum.

I lost count of the amount of times I left the room and went into the kitchen to count to ten, I knew only too well that if I became argumentative then this would only result in upsetting the children even more than they were now.

I was polite, and courteous, and did my very best to show this to Helen, hoping that she would see that myself and Susie were responsible and loving people, and our only concern was the children. As time went by Helen became very officious and unapproachable, it was all I could do at times to get a smile out of her.

Deep down myself and Susie knew that this was going to change our lives forever, there was little we could do to change the situation, and for all intents and purposes if the children agreed, a decision had already been made about their future.

At this point in time Helen said that she would like to 'question' the children about how they felt. The minute she said this I could see the children look over to myself and Susie looking for some type of reassurance.

All I could say to them was 'Kids, just answer Helen honestly. Tell her honestly what you want, you know we have discussed this on lots of occasions and myself and Susie know exactly what you want. So don't be afraid to tell Helen what you want to do'.

To give Helen her due she was good with the children. She smiled, and did her best to make them feel relaxed. But, you could see in the children's faces that they were upset, and in no small measure feeling guilty about what they were about to say.

After the initial conversation Helen asked the children if they were prepared to go back and live with Jennie and Steve? Not a word passed their lips, their eyes were full of tears that started to roll down their faces. All they could do was nod in agreement and then look at myself and Susie and say 'Sorry'.

As I've said, we knew this day would come, but to be faced with such a situation was heartbreaking in the extreme. I'm not normally one to show my emotions, and particularly at this time I was not about to show the children just how upset I was.

There was a feeling in the pit of my stomach that to this day I have never felt since. At times I could not bring myself to look at the kids as I knew if I did I would break down in tears and become uncontrollably sad.

Helen by this time was taking notes, and indeed was recording the conversations that took place. I guess in the world we presently live in this was done as a matter of course, but it did make the situation even worse, if that was all possible.

The interview lasted approximately forty five minutes, and

it was one of the longest forty five minutes I have ever experienced. I would like to say that everything was now out in the open, but to tell you the truth all I wanted to do was for the ground to swallow me up and take away my pain.

The children had been honest and open about their wishes. I imagine they felt as if they had in someway been treacherous to both myself and Susie. In their children's minds I am sure that what they had said to Helen that evening was not only cruel, but also vindictive in someway.

This of course was not the truth, we all knew that the children wanted to go back to Jennie and Steve and there was little else to be said. After all, the children's happiness was our main concern, and if this meant them going back to their mum, then of course this is what had to happen.

I thanked Helen for coming over and asked her what happened next. Once again I was met with officialdom in the extreme. I was told that the report she had written would be submitted to a board, and the results would be given to myself and Susie at a later date.

She also said that the report would be given to Jennie and Steve so that everything was above board, and we could all see what had transpired that evening. I did not have a problem with this, except for the fact that I still wanted to know a little more of what had actually happened at Jennies house.

Helen told me that it was down to Jennie to tell me, if she so wished. Helen apparently could not comment any further, and to do so would be breaching the rules and regulations of social services.

I tried to assimilate and understand this the best way I could, but it was still a situation that was nightmarish. I was asking some very valid questions that revolved around my children's future, I thought that at the very least I should be made aware of any other problems the family had.

Once Helen had gone myself and Susie sat and talked with the children and told them that what they said was OK, and it had to be said. We assured them that their happiness was our main concern and just so long as their mum and Steve could look after them in the future then we did not have a problem with them returning.

If truth were known myself and Susie were virtually bereft of any emotion at this time. It was as if all emotion had been sucked from us, and we were now living, or surviving, as if we were both robots.

We did not want the children to see how upset we both were. We were determined that the children would only see that we were pleased that they had been honest, and that they would soon return to their mums house.

That evening the children went to bed as normal ready for the next day. Myself and Susie didn't say an awful lot to each other after the children went to bed. We both knew that in the not too distant future the children would be taken back to Jennies house and we would once again be left feeling emotionally drained and sick to the very pit of our stomachs.

Myself and Susie were trying to second guess when the children would go back, in reality, we had no idea when this was going to happen, our mindset was one of dejection and sadness.

Ten days later we received a letter from the social services outlining what had transpired that evening, and also informing us that the children were going to go to back to Jennies house the following week, three days before Christmas.

Myself and Susie had often discussed how great it would be to have the children over Christmas, I had never been allowed to see my children on Christmas Day since myself and Jennie separated. I had only been allowed to pick them up on Boxing Day and have them for two or three days.

We thought now, however foolhardy these thoughts, that we may have the children on Christmas Day and we could all spend a lovely time together before they had to go back to Jennies house.

But this was not the case, it had been decided that the

children would go back to their mum three days before Christmas. Myself and Susies dreams were shattered in one brief instant. We had managed to convince ourselves that the children would spend Christmas Day with us, and in our ignorance we had completely ignored the fact that this may not have been the case.

There was little point in making a scene, or indeed kicking up a fuss. To have done so would have caused heartache all around. The last thing we wanted to do was to spoil the children's Christmas, but it was all I could do to stop myself from phoning Jennie and asking why the hell we had to give the children back three days before Christmas?

Susie managed to calm me down in her own incompatible way yet again, and explain to me that if I took such a path then it was I who would pay the price in the future.

We had received the letter informing us of the decision on a weekday when the children were at school, so it was with a heavy heart that myself and Susie had to tell them that they were going back to their mums house on the 22nd December.

As normal, myself and Susie put on a brave face and told the children that to see them back with their mum made us happy, and at least they would be back in their our own house for Christmas.

We had looked after the children for nearly three months by this time, it was indeed an extremely happy time and one that we all enjoyed, bearing in mind the situation back at Jennies house.

The days went by as they do, and each and everyday was counted off the calendar by myself and Susie. We knew only too well that in a couple of days time the children would be going back to their house and we would be left spending Christmas with sadness and the stark silence of no children.

I had been forced away from my children many years ago, I had never really got over this. To be faced with the same situation again was more than I could bear. But for the children's sake I put on a brave face and told them that they had made the correct decision, and whilst we would be sad to see them go, we would soon get back into the routine of seeing each other on weekends once again, and having a laugh and a joke whenever possible.

In truth my heart was broken, the tears that fell from my eyes were non stop when no one was around. I was going to have to face once again saying goodbye to my children for the foreseeable future. I honestly didn't know if I could cope with this, but with Susies help I knew in someway I would get through it.

The 22nd of December dawned like any other day, except for the fact that once again I was having to say goodbye to my children, and I would only be able to see them once every two weeks for the briefest of times.

It was arranged that I would drop the children off at Jennies, as I wanted them to be reassured that I was OK with the situation. Nothing could have been further from the truth, but I needed the children to know in their own minds that everything was OK with the situation.

I had made arrangements with Jennie to drop the children off at noon, as this would give them some more time together to settle down before the evening. Bags were packed, in anticipation of the day ahead.

Susie said that she would stay at home because if she came over as well she knew she would breakdown, and this was the last thing she wanted the children to see. I was in total agreement with her, the last thing I wanted was for the children to become upset, and see Susie breakdown in such a way.

She had been an inspiration to not only me, but my children, she was loving, kind, and giving. She looked after my children as if they were her own and I knew only too well that the sadness and grief she was going to feel was going to be immense.

The journey to Jennies house took an eternity, but I kept the jokes and smiles going all the way to Jennies front door. At no point in time did I ever let the children see how upset and grief stricken I truly was.

I would not allow my children to see how upset I had become. I wanted them to return to Jennies house knowing that dad was alright, and we would all once again soon enough get back into a routine.

As we arrived at Jennies house the front door opened, no one came out to greet us. I guess Jennie and Steve were finding it difficult also. Deep down Jennie must have known, or maybe not, about how I felt about taking the children back.

I had by this time still managed to keep a brave face, though my insides were in turmoil and my stomach felt as if it wanted to explode. The children were in a catch twenty two position, on one hand they knew only too well that by going to live with their mum once again they thought they were being unfair to me and Susie, but on the other hand, they could not wait to rush inside and say hello once again.

I collected my thoughts and did my very best to show the children that they had made the right decision. As I ushered the children from the car all I wanted to do was to scream to the heavens and ask what the hell was going on? But this would have been of no help to anybody, least of all the children.

There was still no one at the front door so it was down to me to try to bring this situation to a conclusion that would make everybody happy, in the worst possible circumstances.

The hugs I gave my children that day were the biggest and most heartfelt I had ever given them. I didn't want to let them go, but I knew deep down that the decision all those concerned had arrived at was a decision that could not be gone back on.

As the children went through the door all I could think to myself was one thing, and one thing alone. That no matter what, I'd had the privilege to share the love once again of my children for the past three months, and nobody could take that away from me.

The drive back home that evening took nearly three hours. I didn't know what I was going to do or say to Susie, and what was going to happen to us both. The children had been a huge part of both our lives, and now they were only going to be part of it every other weekend once again.

The void they left was immense and absolutely dreadful, there was nothing that could possibly fill this void, except Susie.

When I finally arrived home Susie had no real idea of what to say to me, and vise versa. She was after all, extremely upset and was at a loss as to what to say, or indeed do. We both just sat down and cried our eyes out. There was little to say. Nothing said at this point in time would make either of us feel any better.

Soon enough our lives once again returned to some sort of routine, the same routine that we had been used to for many months before. However, we both knew that the hole left in our lives could never be filled.

The children by now were a lot older, 12 and 14 years old, so in essence they had a fair grasp of what had gone on. Each and every weekend we picked them up they would apologise for choosing to live once again with my ex-wife. We explained to them that there was no need to do this as we both understood completely. But the children still felt some pangs of guilt.

It was no good trying to gloss over the situation. Even though myself and Susie were inconsolable, we tried with all our might to never show this to the children.

After all, they were innocent victims in a world where often as adults, we mess up our lives so completely and utterly.

Resentment
****

Life once again seemed very ordinary, or rather I should say, mundane. Myself and Susie no longer had the children in our lives constantly. We were once again faced with a life that was rather empty. That is not to say that we were not happy. We still loved each other as we had always done, if not more so due to what we had experienced.

Through the trials and tribulations of the past few years and months we had become a lot closer. This is often the case when people are faced with experiences that put a strain on any relationship. These strains can either make us, or break us. Fortunately the former was true of myself and Susie.

However, no matter hard we tried the void that the children had left was not going to be easy to fill. Though we were seeing the children every other weekend this was not enough for either of us.

We had often discussed the issue of custody. We had taken legal advice on this matter, and the result was that unless we could prove Jennie was an unfit mother we would stand little chance of getting custody of my children.

Susie would often push me to start the process of a custody battle, but I was fairly reticent to do such a thing. There were several reasons for this. Firstly, as my legal advisor had said, unless I could prove beyond a doubt that Jennie was an unfit mother, I would stand little chance of a positive outcome.

Secondly, was the fact that if I took such a path, in my mind, this would be to the detriment of the children's welfare. As far as I was aware the children had never been at risk from Jennie or Steve. Even though there had been some issues in recent months, at no point in time did my children look and sound as if they were unhappy.

If I were to go to court and win, though this was a very, very, slim possibility, would my children hold it against me in the future? The relationship I had with my children, though loving and caring was at times tenuous, simply because I only got to see them once every two weeks.

I did not want my children now, or in the future to resent me for any action that I took that could be construed as having a go at Jennie. The last ting I wanted to do was put the relationship I had with my children in jeopardy, no matter how small this risk.

I explained this to Susie on numerous occasions and as normal she saw my point of view. She would of however, at the drop of a hat support me if I should ever change my mind.

By this time myself and Susie decided that we would once again return to Australia. This time however it was for different reasons. The situation we know found ourselves in was one of grief and sadness.

We thought that by going out to Australia for several weeks this may give us the opportunity to rebuild our lives and once again carry on. We thought that we deserved this extended holiday so that it may give us the chance to assimilate what had taken place over the past few months.

We did however decide that this time the return to Australia would be somewhat different. We had often spoken about the possibility of showing the children Australia, and this seemed like an ideal time.

Our plan was to gain permission from Jennie and Steve to take the children with us for six weeks. We would hire a camper van and show the children the 'real' Australia. Our plans were to go to Australia during my children's summer holidays so that they didn't miss their education. Once the six weeks were over we would fly back with them and make sure they got home safely.

These plans were very tentative, as I had to ask Jennie if this was OK. I took the bull by the horns and rang Jennie in April, well before the summer holidays were to begin. To my surprise Jennie was in complete agreement and said it was a marvellous idea.

Plans were put into place and the excitement from not only myself and Susie, but also the kids was magnificent. Our tickets were booked and the necessary planning was in full swing.

Three days before our flights were due we received a telephone call from Jennie. The tenure from the outset was one of tension and anger. Jennie informed us that she had changed her mind, and the children were no longer allowed to travel with us.

I asked, or rather demanded an explanation, but there was none. All I was told was that the children were not going to go to Australia with us and that was the end of the discussion. It was all I could do to keep a semblance of rationality.

The monetary aspects of the holiday were of little consequence to us. Yes, it had cost thousands of pounds to organise the trip. The flight costs alone were not refundable, and we had already booked a five berth camper van for our use.

No, these matters concerned us very little. I wanted my children to see our 'home'. Myself and Susie wanted to show them the real Australia. The outback, beaches, rainforest, in fact, all of Australia.

I was at a loss as to what to do next. Susie by this time was trying to calm me down, but there was little she could say or do that would placate me. My next step was one that I should of thought long and hard about, but my state of mind at this time was one of abject rage and disappointment.

I decided that the only course of action available to me was to go to the children's house and demand an explanation. In hindsight this was not such a great idea, but at this time it was thought the correct path to take.

I arrived at the children's house early that evening. I was determined to keep a modicum of politeness for the sake of everybody involved, if this was possible.

I knocked at the front door and was met with a rather stern and argumentative Jennie. I refrained from losing my temper as past history had taught me to tread very carefully. All I asked was why had she done such a thing? The reply was as unbelievable as I could have ever heard.

All Jennie said to me was, 'If you take the children

to Australia I know you will keep them out there'. To say I was amazed would be a travesty. I never, ever had thought such a thing. At no point in time had myself or indeed Susie ever said to each other that our intention was to 'kidnap' the children.

After all, that is what I was being accused of. I was being told that I was not only planning such a thing, but indeed this had been my intention from the outset.

This just went to show how well Jennie knew me. If I were planning such a venture did she not realise that I would not only be destroying her life, but also the lives of the children? I would be taking them away from their mother and this would inevitably lead to the childrens sorrow and sadness.

I didn't know what to say to such an accusation. In actual fact I didn't have the chance to say anything. The next thing I knew was that a police car had arrived at Jennies house and two policeman were approaching me.

Jennie had obviously contacted the police as soon as I had arrived and fabricated a story about me to get me removed. There was little I could do or say. The police by this time had stood between myself and Jennie and one of the officers said to me, 'If you don't mind sir we would like you to leave the premises please'.

You would of thought that I would of said something in return, but no, all I did was to hang my head, turn around and once again get in my car and drive back home. I knew only too well that I was in no way going to win this battle. From previous experiences I knew that the only course of action to take was to walk away with a degree of dignity.

There are no words to explain the atmosphere when I finally returned home. Susie had no idea of what to say or do. We just hugged each other and tried to understand what had just happened, not that any degree of understanding was possible.

Once again I had seen a side of human nature that astounded me. It is true that several phone calls were made during the following days, but these only resulted in nothing being resolved. I was told over and over again that there was no way the children were going to Australia, and if I kept pestering Jennie she would once again inform her solicitor and the police.

We were faced with a situation that was very nearly untenable. I had even asked to speak with the children, but was told that they did not want to speak to me, or indeed go to Australia.

My next actions to the bystander may at first seem rather confusing and slightly shocking. It is true that once again I had the love of my children, even though this was for only every other weekend. I did have them back in my life, for the briefest of moments.

But the disappointment myself and Susie felt were incalculable. We had been looking forward to showing the children the wonders of Australia, and this had now been taken away, so what were we to do?

Myself and Susie once again decided that the best course of action would be to once again return to Australia, not only to give ourselves time to think, but also the holiday had already been booked and if we cancelled at this late date we would receive very little money back because of the late cancellation.

We truly had no idea if this was going to be a long-term plan or indeed just a brief holiday, all we knew was that we would once again return to Australia and see how things transpired.

We told the children of our plans, and to give them their due they understood completely. They knew that the holiday had been booked well in advance and realised that it was foolhardy to cancel at this late stage.

So, with goodbyes said once again we departed the UK and set off for Australia. No matter how many times I travel to Australia it is always like going home. The country and its people never cease to amaze, astound, and it must be said, at times, annoy the hell out of me.

As I have previously said, Australia is not perfect by any stretch of the imagination, but nonetheless it does each and every time welcome me with open arms and asks little of me. Except that I embrace the country and its people, as the country has done with myself.

Heartbreak Once Again
****

Myself and Susie had through our experiences in Australia seen and done a lot of what you could call the 'touristy' things, beaches, sights, wildlife etc, and we were looking forward to showing the children these same sights if they had accompanied us on our trip.

But this was no longer an option, so we decided that we would travel for some time before we came to a decision about our long-term future. We had already booked the camper van, so it would have been silly not to make full use of this. We picked the van up in Sydney and proceeded to drive west, we really had no idea where our trip would take us, all we knew was that we were going to make the most of the time we had the van for.

After some three weeks we had arrived in Albany, Western Australia, we had seen Albany before, but still made the most of our time in this rather quaint city.

As you will be aware myself and Susie when we left for our trip had no idea if this was going to be just a holiday, or a long-term plan. We had after all envisaged my children accompanying us on the trip, you could say we felt somewhat hollow.

We decided after five weeks of being in Australia that we would once again return to the UK and try to make a long-term future for ourselves. If truth were known, we had no idea if this was the best course of action to take, but in all honesty we were left with little choice.

I now had my children back in my life and they had to be my first consideration. The pull of Australia was immense, and at times I did question my motives for going back to the UK. But when all was said and done, the children had to be our main priority, as myself and Susie wanted to build a firm and loving relationship with them after so many years apart.

We arrived back in the UK with the sole intention of making a future life for ourselves. No matter what happened,

Australia was still going to be a huge part of our lives, and this we had little doubt of. But for the foreseeable future our responsibilities lay elsewhere.

As time went by the normal day to day chores were taken care off and myself and Susie soon slipped into a routine where we seemed relatively happy. I was now seeing my children every other weekend once again, though this was not enough, it sufficed at the time.

Myself and Jennie by this time, whilst being communicative, were still very weary of each other. I was only too aware that the relationship I now had with my children could be put at risk by anything said and done.

However, our lives soon got into a routine, and the normal day to day activities that we all have to do to make a life for ourselves went by as normal.

It was now May of 2007, myself and Susie had been together for nearly eight years. We had often discussed the subject of marriage, and we both thought that our relationship was such that to get married was the next obvious step. We both loved each other very much, and to confirm this by getting married was something that we both were looking forward to.

So in August of 2007 myself and Susie got married, it was a happy and very proud day, and it is a day that I shall remember with fond and happy memories.

By this time Susies job was going very well, she enjoyed her work immensely and was indeed an excellent attribute to her employers. My driving instructor career, whilst being somewhat repetitive, did give me the opportunity to meet different people everyday, and I was relatively happy in my chosen career path.

Maybe it is because I am a 'man' that at times I cannot see what is staring me in the face. But, around November of 2007 I noticed a small change in Susies demeanour. I couldn't quite put my finger on it, but nonetheless it was somewhat worrying.

Whilst the change wasn't immense I noticed that Susie didn't laugh or talk to me as much as she used to. I put this down to the stress of her work, and also the fact that at times I had to work very long hours. But, nonetheless it was a worrying facet of our newly married life.

Whilst I didn't ignore the change in Susie, I did try and put it to the back of my mind. This could have been for several reasons. Not least the fact that I had seen a change in Jennie before, and this had in the long-term, lead to our marriage breakdown.

So if truth were known, I guess to some extent I refused to acknowledge the change in Susie and carried on as if nothing out of the ordinary was taking place. But, as time went by it was a worrying facet of my life.

One evening myself and Susie were sitting down after having our evening meal and she asked me if she could have a chat with me. Ordinarily, Susie would never have asked such a thing, we had the type of relationship that was very open and honest, if we needed to talk about something then normally we would just come out and say it.

But this was different, Susie looked very serious when she had asked me for a chat, and to say I was worried would be an understatement.

I asked her what was the matter, as I did I could see in her face that what she was about to say was going to have a massive impact on my future life. I by this time was becoming very worried as I had seen this type of behaviour before with Jennie. Surely Susie, the woman I love with all my heart was not about to do the same thing?

It was all I could do to try and relax and explain to Susie that no matter what she said, I would listen, and if at all possible help. But I could see in her face that she knew what she was about to say would be met with astonishment and great sadness.

I cannot remember the whole conversation, but I do however remember the very first few sentences. Susie said to me, 'I want a divorce, I've had enough'. My reaction was off shock and amazement. As I said, I cannot remember the whole conversation, but I did ask Susie exactly what she meant.

Whilst I had heard Susies words, I guess that somewhere in my subconscious I had refused to acknowledge them. Surely she couldn't have said what she just did? I pleaded with her to try and explain more fully exactly what she meant.

By this time her eyes were streaming with tears and it was all she could do to even look at me. She went on to explain that while she still loved me, she didn't love me as once she had. I couldn't understand exactly what she was trying to say to me, it was all I could do to meet her eye, and try for the life of me to make sense of what was being said.

By this time I was what you could call bereft of any emotion. I was numb, dumbfounded and shocked as to what Susie had just said. I couldn't compute the information that was coming my way, in fact, it was all I could do to remain focused.

However, Susie went on to try and explain her thoughts and emotions. She told me that she was enjoying her job immensely, and indeed she was in line for a promotion. With this in mind, she said that she wanted to put some 'roots' down, and just by being married to me she was not going to be able to do this.

I begged her to explain more fully so that I could have some semblance of understanding. This last statement I didn't understand at all, and needed to clarify exactly what she was saying. I had after all, done my best in the past to take a keen interest in her job, and what she was doing.

She had come to the conclusion that myself and Australia were if you like, one entity, and she could never see Australia not being a part of my life. This she felt would always get in the way of our relationship. She thought, rightly or wrongly, that Australia and its people would always be an obstacle in our future relationship.

In other words what she was trying to say to me was simply this. She had now found a career with a long-term future that she was doing very well in, and she thought that if she remained married to me this would in someway jeopardise said career.

She did her best to explain in her own way, but no matter what she said I could not fully comprehend what she meant. She further went on to explain that no matter what happened in our future, Australia would always be there, and in some way get in the way of any long-term happiness she could have.

I could understand completely the need for her to put down roots, and settle into a way of life that most people do so in their day to day lives. And I guess, I can also understand what she was trying to say about Australia and myself. Yes, Australia had been a big part of my life in the past, present, and would be in the future, but at no point in time would I let Australia jeopardise our marriage.

I explained to her that in order for her to be happy then of course I would settle permanently in the UK, in so doing I hoped this would help her come to a different decision. I went on to tell her that no matter what, her happiness was of paramount importance to me, if this meant us remaining in the UK forevermore then that was fine. I also said to her that just because we may make the decision to stay in the UK that does not mean we could never travel back to Australia once or twice a year.

Susie would hear little of it, she said to me that if we chose to stay in the UK then she knew only too well that this would lead to my long-term unhappiness, and I would one day turn this unhappiness around and blame her for making me stay in the UK.

I said this was not true, at no point in time now, or in the future, would I ever blame her for making me stay in the UK. I was after all, a grown adult. I could make my own decisions, good or bad. If it meant Susie was to be happy then of course I would stay in the UK, I could still maintain a relationship with Australia, however tenuous, and this would make everyone happy.

But she would hear little of it. She insisted that no matter what happened in the future I would at some point blame her for not living in Australia. She was adamant that she had come to the correct decision, and even though it was upsetting, it was a decision that she knew was right.

By this stage, I was tired and exhausted. After all, we had only been married for some three months and I asked myself this one question, 'Why hadn't Susie told me of her feelings before we got married? To me, she must have been feeling this way for some time, so why only now did she feel it right to tell me?

I couldn't comprehend what had just been said. I asked her how long she had been feeling this way, but unfortunately there was no response.

Susie by this time was extremely upset and to tell you the truth was not making a lot of sense. All she kept saying was that Australia and its people would always play a huge part of my life, and this would in turn play a huge part in her life.

She had come to the stage in her life where she wanted to make a long-term future for herself in England, her job was going extremely well, and she had come to realise that if she remained with me, her long-term happiness would be put in jeopardy.

I once again begged and pleaded with her to listen to what I was saying. That Australia could still be a part of our lives even if we remained in the UK. I was not going to allow Australia and its people to come between us, and I would indeed sacrifice any long-term future I had with Australia for the sake of Susie and her happiness. But this was to no avail. She would hear little of it, and just kept saying that in order for her to be happy we would have to separate and eventually divorce.

By this time I was feeling drained and didn't really understand what had just taken place. My mind was totally confused and in a state of utter devastation. I had told Susie that whilst Australia would always play a huge part in my life I would always put her feelings first, and if this meant not returning to Australia on a permanent basis then that was fine.

I knew in my heart of hearts that what I was saying was

true, I would have willingly stayed and lived in the UK if this would make Susie happy. We both had a relatively good jobs that would enable us to go out to Australia at least once a year, and this I thought would be enough.

We had after all, decided to come back to the UK to form a loving relationship with my children. So in essence I was more than prepared to do the same for Susie.

Susie was sure in her own mind that Australia would always play a huge part of my life, and to some extent she would always be in competition with the country and its people.

In no small measure she was correct, of course Australia and its people would always play a huge part of my life. Australia had been there for me when I thought that nothing else was. She had never hurt me, or gone out of the way to hurt me. Australia and its people would always play a huge part of my life. But the part it had to play in my future life was going to have to be different now.

I was prepared at that time to sacrifice my feelings for Australia in order for myself and Susie to live and work in the UK. Whilst I was extremely sad at such a decision, I was prepared to make it for all our sakes.

Trying To Carry On
****

I won't go into too much detail of the weeks that followed Susies decision. Suffice to say, that there were many tears, conversations, arguments, tantrums, and an overriding atmosphere of great sadness. I had once again had the love of a woman taken away from me, and now I was left with a feeling of complete emptiness and sadness that I had felt many years before when myself and Jennie separated.

I had lost what I was in life, a husband. That was what I was, a husband who I thought, had shown love, support, and caring to their partner. Now once again I was just an empty shell, I had no idea of where to turn.

I had lost yet again the love that made me whole. The strange thing is this. That throughout my adolescence and indeed adult life, I had never been the one to end a relationship. In truth, I never saw the need to. At no point in time had I been the one to turn to my partner/wife and ask that the relationship come to an end.

That is not to say that my relationships in my eyes were perfect, indeed, at times they were far from it. But this was never enough reason to make me come to the conclusion that the relationship was over. I thought, however foolishly, that any problems could be overcome, and the relationship would continue.

In no way, shape, or form by saying this am I blaming the other party in any relationship I have ever had. Nothing could be further from the truth. At that time in 'their' lives the reasons they gave for wanting the relationship to end were valid, thorough, and thought best for them. For this I do not blame them at all.

However, because I was the one being asked to leave the relationship I was in other words being told that I was no longer loved and had to 'stop' loving the other party.

It's difficult to explain, but I will do my best. When in your eyes there is nothing wrong with the relationship then the love you feel for your partner is as strong as it ever was. To be told that you are no longer wanted in a relationship is in other words being told that you are no longer loved, or at least, not loved in the same way as you once were.

To be faced with this scenario can be nightmarish in proportions. To be told that the love and compassion you once felt from the other person is now non-existent, or minimal in its appearance, is indeed a very bitter pill to swallow.

Secondly, is this fact, and it is probably even worse than the first emotion I have outlined. Though it is still very difficult to accept that the other person may not love you in the same way, the even more horrific fact to face is this.

That in order for the other party, and indeed yourself to move on, you have to try and stop loving the other person concerned. How on Gods green earth do you do this when all you know is the fact that the love you still feel is as strong as ever?

If you cannot convince yourself to stop loving the other party the emotions and heartbreak you feel will be magnified one hundred fold. How do you now live a life that does not include the love you felt for your chosen partner in life?

After all, that is what makes you a human being. Your very being is the 'love' you had for this person. That's all you are. What makes you the person you are is simply the love you felt for your now 'absent' partner.

How do you wake each morning, how do you sleep at night, how do you continue with life, indeed, how do you exist, now that you have been told that you have to 'stop' loving the other person?

You have to stop loving purely to continue living. How on earth is this done? I wish I had the answer, but I do not. In point of fact, I don't think I will ever find the answer.

It is not a switch that can be turned on and off. I wish it was as simple as that. But somewhere, you have to find the answer. If you do not, your life will be nightmarish in its existence.

As I said, I have never found the answer. It has taken me many years to come to terms with my relationship failings, and in many respects I still haven't come to terms with many aspects of my relationship breakdowns.

The vast majority of my life now, I live happily and contentedly. But there are days when an overwhelming feeling of emptiness pervades, and I look back at the different types of love I have experienced and still miss the person involved immensely.

These days are very rare indeed, but they occasionally sneak up on me when I least expect them, and they take me back to a time when my world imploded. When I felt absolutely heartbroken.

If I were truthful I am thankful for these days. Because they show me that I am still a functioning human being. I can now look back at these times and realise the experiences and emotions I felt made me into the person I am today.

Whether this is a good or bad thing, you would have to ask those that know and love me now.

A Better Place
****

I had already moved out of the marital home as I thought this the best course of action to stop any further upset. I still spoke to Susie fairly regularly, each conversation involved me asking her to reconsider her decision. I told her time and time again that no matter what, if we were to stay married then everything would be OK, and we could build a future for ourselves in England.

But Susie would hear little of it. She never became nasty or vindictive, the opposite in fact. But she was certain that at her long-term future was in England, and she thought that if we remained married she would be stopping me from the life she thought I wanted in Australia.

Nothing I said or did convinced her otherwise, at no point in time was she ever going to reconsider her decision. I had just lost my rock that had found me at my worst ever low in Australia. She had been there for me, picked me up, and given me the strength to go on.

But now that rock had gone, and once again it was all I could do to raise myself from bed each morning and try and get on with another day. The overriding emotion I had was one of complete emptiness.

My family once again were my salvation. My parents in no small measure played a massive part in the following weeks. They were as ever, there with support and compassion that only loving parents can show. For this I am eternally grateful, and no words I ever say, or write can encompass just what my parents and family mean to me.

It was obvious that my marriage was beyond repair, no matter how hard I tried, no matter how much begging I made to Susie, my life was once again that of a single man and it was something I was going to have to get used to yet again.

I did however phone Jennie and tell her of the situation. She was understanding and compassionate in all that she said. She even asked if I wanted to go over to her house and talk things through. Whilst I appreciated this offer I thought it best if I keep myself to myself as I thought this was the best course of action to take.

Whilst I was bereft of what had happened, the children were now faced with a prospect of a future without Susie in it. Susie had always been a loving step mum, she had shown my children so much love and care that to this day I am truly thankful.

They could understand a little of what had gone on. I did my best to explain to them what had happened, and yet again was adamant in my decision not to apportion blame. At no point in time was I about to criticise Susie for the decision she had come to. I did in actual fact tell the children that if truth were known the majority of fault for my marriage breakdown was mine, and mine alone.

If I had made Susie feel the way she did then there was no one else to blame but myself. The children as ever would hear little of it, and in no small measure took their anger and frustration out on each other. I made it quiet clear that they should never speak to Susie about the reasons behind the marriage breakdown.

I felt that anything they said would not only upset them, but also Susie. I told them that adults make mistakes all the time, and at times these mistakes can seem catastrophic.

But these mistakes are things in life that we all have to deal with, and one day in the future we would all be able to repair the damage that had been done, and once again carry on with our lives.

It was at this point in time that I decided to try and change my life radically. I dare say a lot of people go through such thoughts and emotions when a breakdown of a relationship takes place.

The reasons are at times a little difficult to fathom. Maybe it is the need to metamorphose into someone completely different. Maybe it is the need for 'closure', I hate that word, but it is one that I feel justified in using in this particular instance. And to this day I still do not know why I chose to take such a path, but at the time I felt this avenue of human nature was right for me.

I decided however foolishly, that I was going to get myself super fit again, and attempt to give up smoking. I knew this wasn't going to be easy, but nonetheless I thought I would give it a go.

By this time I was staying at a friends flat. He was away on business and the property he left behind would of stood vacant for some three months if I had not been staying there.

My friend suggested that I should stay there as I could look after the care and maintenance of the property and he could also trust me implicitly.

Even though my family begged me to stay with them I would hear little of it. I had after all on many occasions stayed with my parents and I could not in all conscience do this again. Besides I thought to myself, 'I need to get used to living by myself, and it may give me the opportunity to ajust a lot quicker to this new phase of my life'. How wrong I was.

I knew from past experience that to give up smoking was going to be extremely difficult. I had before tried every non-smoking aid that was on the market. Some had worked, to a degree, whilst others failed miserably, or rather, I had failed miserably.

But by this point in time there was a new drug on the market that by all accounts seemed to be a 'wonder' drug that would lead to a smoke free life.

I took myself off to the doctors and asked if this new drug may be of use to me. The doctor talked to me at great length about the drug in question, and for all intense and purposes was very detailed in his advice.

He did however ask me one very important question. And it was this. 'Was I at the present time under any degree of depression, or of a negative frame of mind'? His reasons for asking this question were simple.

The drug concerned, though no actual 'proof' was evident, had been linked to several suicides in the past by some patients who were already slightly depressed.

I realise that the actions I took next were wholly irresponsible, arrogant, selfish and contemptible, but my mindset at that time was one of absolute determination, and an overriding will to change my life, completely.

I answered the doctors question in the negative. Of course I wasn't depressed, my life was happy, and I was looking forward to the challenge of becoming a non-smoker. If I had been thinking logically I would of given a wholly different answer. But that is the point, I was not thinking logically, at all.

So with prescription in hand I left the doctors office sound in the knowledge that I was going to become not only fitter, but also a non-smoker.

The flat where I was staying was very nice. It was comfortable, and clean. However, it was slightly sterile and not very homely. I was by this time working very long hours in the hope that this would take my mind off the separation from Susie.

This was to little avail though, as constant thoughts of the life I previously had were all encompassing. No matter how many hours I worked I was still faced with the prospect of going back to my new abode, alone and very, very, lonely.

I had been on the new wonder drug for approximately five days, whilst they stopped completely and utterly the cravings for a cigarette I did find that they caused some rather strange side effects.

Or was I wrong in this first interpretation? Each evening I would cook, or rather microwave, my evening meal and each time I ate, an overwhelming feeling of absolute desperation and sadness would surround me.

I would often sit there with tears rolling down my face and there was little I could do to stem the flow. I do not know why this particular feeling was so devastating at meal times. I felt throughout the day very depressed, but when I ate my evening meal the emotion I felt grew tenfold.

In no small measure I put these feelings down to the separation that had taken place between myself and Susie, but I still had enough commonsense remaining to realise that maybe, just maybe, the drug I was on for stopping smoking may have been having an effect.

I did for this reason stop taking the drug that evening. Even then, when I was at a very low ebb, I had enough common sense to realise that the wonder drug may be having an effect, no matter how small. I was still adamant that I was not about to start smoking again, and thought I could do this without the aid of drugs!

The next morning I woke, and I realise that what I am about to say next, will to some of you, seem weak, irresponsible, irrational, cruel, and wholly unforgivable.

But please try and withhold judgement ever so slightly if at all possible. I woke the next morning with one thought on my mind and one thought only. That life was no longer worth living. I had an overwhelming sense that my life had no meaning any more.

I had often read reports of people trying to kill themselves, and the vast majority of them each and every time said the same thing. That nothing, absolutely nothing else was on their mind except for the fact that they wanted to end their lives.

As a bystander to these events the first thought that would cross my mind when I read or heard such a report was to question the motives of such people.

How can what they say be true? The vast majority of them had people who loved and cared for them in their lives. These people who loved and cared for them would be totally devastated and shocked at what the 'selfish' and 'cowardly' individuals had done.

That is how I viewed people who committed suicide in the past. As cowards and selfish individuals. How dare they even contemplate suicide when their loved ones would be left behind feeling guilt for what had happened?

How dare you commit suicide when there are far more people in the world who are far worse off than you? How dare you commit suicide when you have young children that you are going to leave behind? How dare you put them through this misery for the rest of their lives, because you couldn't be bothered to pick yourself up and get on with life? Grow up you pathetic excuse for a human being.

That is how I viewed those that committed suicide 'before' I felt the emotions and feelings that I was now feeling at this stage in my life.

But that fateful morning I can in all honesty say that I had no other thought on my mind except the need to end my life. No other thought at all. I do not know off any other way of trying to convince you that what I say is true.

At no point in time did I think of anyone, or anything else. I cannot put into words just exactly what I mean. All I can say is that when I woke up that morning it was as if I was in a pit. A pit that was so deep and dark that I could not see out of it. It was as though I had blinkers on, and those blinkers did not let me see anything other than misery and depression.

I can remember this day as if it were yesterday. I woke at six fifteen, I had a very early driving lesson booked in. As I rose from bed I calmly and methodically went into the kitchen, made myself a cup of tea, took the wonder drug from the cupboard and went and sat down in the armchair.

I lit a cigarette, sipped my tea, and ever so calmly and methodically counted the pills I had left. There were twenty two in the box, more than enough to do the deed I thought. After having finished my second cigarette I made yet another cup of tea and lit another cigarette.

I then went and sat back in the armchair and with each gulp of tea, I swallowed a tablet. In between taking the tablets I would take a drag on my cigarette. There was no panic, no retching. In actual fact I was at one of the calmest moments in my life that I had ever been. A feeling of absolute serenity seemed to encompass me.

There was no panic, no tears, no happiness, no sadness, in actual fact, no emotion whatsoever. I know that is difficult to imagine, having no emotions at all. Surely that is what makes us human, emotion?

But at that time in my life I felt nothing at all. You would of thought that there would be emotions attached to such a life changing scene, but there were none. To this day I have never felt the same. I have since then, felt many emotions, in many different ways. Love, compassion, happiness, hate, anger, contentment, are all emotions that subconsciously we all have, twenty four hours a day.

Think about it. At no point in time do we normally feel completely emotionless. Even if we are just sitting watching television, happy in our own space, then the emotions we are feeling are of contentment and relaxation. We may not realise this is happening, but just think about it for a while and I think you will agree with what I am saying.

So for me to say that I was emotionless could be looked at very skeptically. But I can assure you that at that point in time the only thing on my mind was ending my life. And at that time the decision I had come to required very little thought. I just woke that morning and the only thought I had was to end my life, that was the only 'emotion' I was feeling.

That I would be better off dead at this stage in my life. I was no use to anybody. I had let my children down by being a bad dad, I had let Jennie down by being a bad husband, I had let Susie down by being yet again, a bad husband, and I had let my parents and brothers down by always relying on them to get me through the difficult times in my life.

Nothing else mattered, nothing. Any reasoned thought was just not there. No thoughts that I would be leaving two children alone in this world, no thoughts of leaving Jennie with the guilt she would feel. No thoughts of leaving Susie with these same feelings of guilt. No thought that my parents would be left without their son in their lives. No thoughts that my brothers would be left without me.

None, absolutely none of these thoughts ever crossed my mind. I was for all and intense and purposes the only person left on earth, and nothing else mattered. Nothing was going to stop me from taking my own life.

However, after two hours, three more cups of tea, and at least ten cigarettes nothing was happening. All I was feeling was somewhat nauseas because of the amount of cigarettes I had smoked, my caffeine consumption, and a feeling of abject depression.

There was no pain, no urge to fall asleep, nothing, absolutely nothing was happening. I thought that at the very least I would have an overwhelming urge to sleep, or maybe feel some degree of pain. But there was nothing happening.

After another hour I could not understand what was happening. Surely I asked myself, I took enough tablets to do the deed? As I said previously, I am not one for normally taking pills or potions, and in as much did not have any such medication in the house.

If I had, I would of taken these tablets by now and my life would of ended. But I had no such tablets in the house and was by this stage utterly confused.

It was now approaching 9:30 a.m when the phone rang. I picked up the phone and on the other end of the line was my pupil that I was meant to pick up at seven thirty. All I could do was apologise to the young chap concerned and tell him there had been a problem with the car, and I would not be able to see him today.

He was understanding and polite, which I admit is more than I would have been if I had been him. After all, I had let him down tremendously.

However, the result of that phone call was simple. The very fact that somebody had spoken to me when I was feeling as I did came like a bolt from the blue. All of a sudden I came to realise what I had done, and in no small measure, I was scared stiff.

My next course of action was simple. I took myself down to my local doctor and informed the receptionist what I had done. Within a matter of minutes I was rushed to hospital and poked and prodded by the doctors on duty.

I told them what I had done and from here they went about doing their duty. I was immediately hooked up to an ECG machine and several needles and paraphernalia were placed into my arm. I asked what was going on and was told that a doctor would be round to see me fairly soon.

I was by this time still feeling no ill effects, except for a very slight chest pain. Nothing major, but it was definitely uncomfortable.

The doctor then appeared and began to tell me what was going to happen. Apparently, the drugs I had taken, whilst being very strong, only affected the nervous system. They did not affect internal organs at all. After all, the purpose of this drug was to block the signals to the brain that crave nicotine.

Whilst they obviously had to be digested by the stomach there was nothing within the drugs ingredients that would harm any internal organ to any great degree.

However, there was a possibility that my heart could be put under pressure due to the fact that my blood pressure was now through the roof. This was probably due to the fact that in order for the drug to circulate, and my rather excited state, my heart was having to work a lot harder.

By this time I was somewhat bemused. I was however of the mindset that what I had done was not only very stupid, but I was also of the mind that I could not even kill myself properly.

Trust me to pick the one drug that would not affect my internal organs. I had to be the numpty that chose a drug that had the opposite affect of what I wanted it to do. All it did was to make me feel even more depressed that I couldn't have a cigarette until I had been taken off these bloody machines.

I will not go into detail about what happened after this stay in hospital. There were counsellors involved, social workers, and all in all a whole plethora of health workers that wanted to make sure I was in a fit state to go home.

They described what I had gone through as a 'catastrophic mental breakdown'. They spoke at great length about the causes of such an experience, but to tell you the truth I was all to well aware of what had caused this to happen, but nonetheless it was good to speak to those expert in their field, and they did go someway near helping me.

After having lived through such an ordeal I can now in some very, very, small way understand why some people choose to end their lives. We are all different, we all have our very own 'breaking' points. To say I understand each and everyones reasons for wanting to end their own lives would be a gross exaggeration. But what I have learnt through bitter personal experience is that at times the will to carry on living is too much to bear, for some.

Please do not misinterpret what I have just said. Not for one second would I recommend taking the same path as I did. At the end of the day there is always something worth living for, always. But when the depths of desperation do come upon you, it is very difficult to see this point of view, no matter how hard we may try. But I can assure you that though it may not be obvious, there is always something to hold onto and make us want to live.

As I said, the health care system wanted to make sure I was in a fit state to go home. In all honesty I was in no fit state to go home, but as far as wanting to kill myself went, nothing was further removed from my now clearer mind. I remember sitting on the edge of the hospital bed and slowly coming to realise what I had tried to do.

Pictures of my childrens faces were placed squarely at the forefront of my mind, Jennie, Susie, my parents, brothers, friends, all their faces were now the only thoughts I was having. I broke down uncontrollably, and I wept for many hours, and days.

From that moment in time I knew things had to change if I was not about to go down the same path at any future time. All I knew was that I had to do all I could to make myself 'better'.

A New Perspective
****

I was by this time once again staying with my parents, it was after all, just after Christmas and I wanted desperately to be surrounded by those I loved and cared about. As was normal, I got to see my girls on Boxing Day and they stayed with myself and parents for five days.

I was still at this time feeling as if my world had been shattered and it was important to me to have those around me that I knew would not judge or castigate me.

My contract by this time had nearly expired with the driving school and I came to a decision about my short-term future. I decided that once the contract had expired I would go to Australia once again to try and get a semblance of normality back into my life.

I explained this to Jennie, Susie, the children, and my parents, and they all understood to a greater or lesser extent the reasons behind my decision. I had no idea what I was going to do once in Australia. All I knew was that the surroundings I found myself in now were all too familiar, each time I turned around I was faced with something that would remind me of the love that myself and Susie once shared.

At times this was too much to bear, so I thought it best if I take myself out of this situation and try and get my life in some sort of order, no matter how small this was going to be.

I knew I wasn't going to be in Australia for an extended period of time, just enough time to help me get my head sorted out. All I knew was that Australia had never turned its back on me before, and I hoped it wouldn't once again.

Without going into too much detail about this latest trip to Australia I will give you the barest outline of what happened. Before I decided to arrive in Australia I was determined to travel a bit. Unreasonable, maybe, after all I had two children in the UK that 'may' have needed me. It was a decision made on the spur of the moment, and for better or worse, a decision I alone had taken.

Suffice to say that the adventures I had would take a whole other book to explain in any great detail, and maybe one day, I will write such a book.

I visited eighteen countries in total and had experiences, both fightening and wonderful. I was shot at in Bali, had drugs thrust at me in South America, was beaten and stabbed in Johannesburg, had a major car accident in the Phillipines, and at one stage, found myself on a cargo ship in a force nine gale in the middle of pacific ocean, with no recollection of how I got there!

As I said, these stories are for another time, but what I hope you appreciate is that when I finally got to Australia I was becoming a totally different person through the experiences I had been through.

I arrived in Perth and once again knew little of what the future held. I bought an extremely old camper van that was barely road worthy, and drove up the north west coast in the hope that this would bring back some degree of sanity to me.

Rightly or wrongly, I found myself at a place that to this day I look back upon with fond memories. In total I was in Australia for seven weeks. Five of those seven weeks were spent camping in the outback having little contact with anything or anyone.

As I've said, I am not a particularly spiritual person, but during these five weeks I can honestly say that I found some kind of peace and salvation in the stark, desolate environment that is the 'outback'.

The only contact I had with humans was when I went to a service station in the middle of nowhere to stock up on provisions for the camper van. I would often come up to a makeshift campsite on the side of the road many hundreds of miles away from any kind of civilisation. The only contact I had with other people was when a fellow camper or traveller past my way, and we would exchange pleasantries.

I wanted total and absolute isolation. Isolation is completely different to loneliness. From past experience I knew only too well the difference. Loneliness is when you find yourself in the darkest recesses of human existence. Where your every waking moment is one of despair and depression. When you feel as if there is little left to live for, and to carry on would be an injustice.

Isolation is a wholly different animal. It is a place where you can at times, face your fears and find an inner strength to carry on. Isolation is a place of extreme calm and serenity. Where the need to be by oneself is the most powerful emotion we will ever feel. It is a place that at times, is the only place that will help get us through.

So please do not confuse the two. One is a place that few of us would ever want to be, the other is a place where maybe, at some point in our lives, we all 'need' to be.

I did not want to interact with anybody else. I just wanted to see if I could find some sort of peace within my own consciousness.

The days and nights spent in the outback were days and nights unlike any other. I have never experienced such emotions or feelings since that time. The complete and utter peacefulness, isolation, and lack of human contact was a life changing experience.

Until you have experienced such emotions they are difficult to put into words. But I found in the outback some reason to carry on living, and in a way found out who I really was.

I am not saying I went to the outback to 'find' myself. That was never my intention. I just knew that I needed to be completely isolated, and discard any human contact I was to have, at least in the short-term.

As I said, I spent five weeks in north west Australia and those five weeks have proven to me to this present day that there is indeed a 'higher being'. I have no idea what form this higher being has taken, but I am sure in my own mind that at some point, something, or someone was looking after me at this time.

Spiritual, cathartic, cleansing, whatever words I use

can in no way encompass just what this time meant to me. To wake up to the sound of nothing, absolutely nothing except for the occasional kookaburra or crow was indeed a life changing experience.

I had experienced the outback before, but this was different. The experiences and thoughts I had during these five weeks have remained with me to this day. The outback to me is the true Australia. A land that whilst unforgiving, and inhospitable, is also a land of great comfort and compassion.

And inanimate object I agree, but somewhere deep within the outback there is a sense of absolute peace and contentment. To be surrounded by the red dust, gum trees and desert sun was, and is, a feeling of complete joy and fulfillment. Somewhere out there in the stark beauty that is the outback there is a 'soul'. A living, breathing soul that will welcome and embrace those of us that have had the good fortune to spend a little time out there.

As I've said, I am not normally spiritual, but the five weeks spent in the outback have made me realise that there is indeed a bigger picture, and someone, or something has instigated this bigger picture for the betterment of our own souls.

Some of you will say that I am being somewhat 'airy fairy' when I talk of the outback, but my experiences during this time have made me come to realise that no matter what happens in my life, I found during those five weeks a reason for life, no matter what that life brings.

Maybe it was the fact that I had very few possessions with me, after all, the only necessities of life I needed were the basic provisions of food, water, and yes, I admit, cigarettes.

I had absolutely nothing else. When you live life like this you come to realise that what is truly important in life are those around you, those that you love and care about. Not the so-called necessities of everyday living.

I admit that such items as cars, holidays, TV's, dvds, indeed many of the things that we surround ourselves with in this modern day world seem to make our lives more pleasurable, but what I learnt during my time in the outback was simply this.

That if all these things were taken away from me tomorrow I know that in my heart of hearts that I would still be OK, and my life would carry on, regardless.

The reason for this is simplicity in the extreme. No matter the so-called luxuries of our time, the aforementioned items, if these were taken from me for any reason, then I would survive. The reason for this is that I would still have the love, and indeed love, those people that I hold dear in my life.

Maybe its not until you have had experiences as I have had in the past that you begin to realise what is truly 'important' in life. I am not for one second saying that inanimate objects are not important, that would be most unfair of me.

All I am saying is that you could strip away all of the so called 'peripheral, things in my life and I would still be able to function as a caring, loving, compassionate, difficult, arrogant, ignorant, selfish, human being. Just so long as I had the love and support of all those around me.

And yes, I realise that in the description I just gave of myself I included several negative aspects of my personality. That was just being honest, that's all. We all have sides to our character that not only we, but all those around us find somewhat unappealing, but these aspects of ourselves are what make us human beings. To think otherwise is not only foolish, but also very dishonest.

We have to accept the positives as well as the negatives of our makeup if we are too truly understand what makes us human beings.

In coming to the conclusion I did whilst I was in the outback I came to the realisation that we all act at times in a way that those around us cannot understand. Though I had lost Jennie, my children, and Susie in the past I came to a conclusion that was at the time even surprising to me.

That at times people act in a way that seems vindictive, cruel, and selfish. But at other times we all act with love, compassion and care. Maybe not always in equal measure, but nonetheless, we do act as I have just said.

So in essence what I am trying to say is this. That whilst some of the people in my life had acted in a way I found unappealing, they also acted at other times, with love. When they showed me their love I was only too willing to accept and embrace this behaviour. But when they acted in a way that I saw as cruel it was very difficult for me to accept.

What I discovered in the outback was that if I accepted totally, peoples love and support then I had to also accept that at times these same people could also act cruelly. I had to accept the positives and negatives of peoples personalities, in equal measure.

After all, the above emotions are what make us all part of the human race. I now understood why certain people in my life had acted in a way that I found very unappealing. But this is the important part. They only acted in this way because they thought that at the time what they said and did was right for them.

They hadn't gone out of there way to hurt or destroy me. They were just doing what they thought was right at the time, for them. I may not of understood this at the time, but now I was beginning to find some degree of acceptance.

If we as human beings are only too willing to embrace the nicer side of human nature, then we also have to accept that at times, people can act in a way that we find abhorrent.

I am not speaking of many actions that we as humans take. Murder, child molestation, rape, terrorism. These are actions that the vast majority of us find incomprehensible. No, what I am speaking of is the way we all act with each other in our day to day lives.

When we interact with each other there will be times when we find something, someone does, or says very, very unattractive. We cannot at times find a reason for this behaviour. But in the next breath we are only to willing to accept the more positive side to a particular person.

I wish I could say things were different. That we could all get along in this hectic world of ours, without a crossed word ever being said. But this is to live in a 'nirvana'. There is no such place on Gods green earth.

That is not to say that even to this day I look upon everyone I meet with affection and love. At times I still want to rally against what someone has said or done to me. And at times those people that I want to rally against are the ones in my life that are very important to me.

But what I have found since spending a significant amount of time in the outback is that I am far more accepting of peoples behaviour. I may not like, or indeed understand their behaviour, but I have learnt to look beyond the initial facade and try to understand a little more about why certain people act in such a way.

And if I was being brutally honest I would have to admit that at times in my life I have not only acted with love, care and compassion, but I have also acted in a selfish and callous way. Where would I be today if some of the people in my life had only ever seen this negative side of me?

Yes, it's true that certain people only ever wanted to see this side of my character, and in so doing they are no longer part of my life. But the people who took the time and effort to see both sides of my character are those that are still in my life. And for this I can never thank them enough.

It is very difficult to put into words what I am trying to say. I could get all deep and meaningful, and explain my conscious now as being in a state of 'enlightenment' or 'fulfillment'. But that would be an over exaggeration in the extreme.

If I had indeed found enlightenment or fulfillment then the times I find myself filled with anger and frustration would indeed be far less. I still at times find myself questioning some peoples actions. To me their actions are at times inexcusable. So to say I have found any such 'higher' plain would be pathetic.

All I know is that at this moment in my life I can honestly say that I am a far better person than I was many years ago. Not perfect by any stretch of the imagination. I still have many, many faults that not only I find distasteful, but also all those around me find distasteful. But I am now, at least the vast majority of the time, a more caring and compassionate individual.

In no small measure I have to thank the experiences I have gone through that have bought me to this place in my life. I may not of liked or understood what was going on at the time, but now everything is a lot clearer and I can now grasp what my life has tried to teach me, good and bad.

The one experience that I have to thank in most part is the time I spent in the outback those many years ago. I never arrived there thinking that it would change me radically, all I knew at the time was that I needed to find some kind of peace, just for a while.

But the five short weeks spent there was an experience that I shall never forget. To walk through its red deserts alone, yet to walk these same deserts surrounded. To touch the vast emptiness and feel nothing, yet to touch again and feel everything. To be surrounded by complete nothingness, yet be enveloped by this nothingness. To look toward the sunrise and see nothing, yet to look again and see everything. To look up at the vast blue and imagine little, yet to look again and imagine all. To sleep at night and hear silence, yet to sleep again and hear everything. To look up at the stars and feel so isolated, yet to look again and feel so comforted. To wake in the morning and feel such a void, yet to wake again and be enriched by this void. To feel all your senses so nullified, yet feel all your senses come so alive.

I cannot possibly convey to you what those five weeks meant to me, I hope I have in some small measure done so within this chapter. If I have not achieved this then maybe the experiences I did have during those five weeks are indeed inexplicable, and well beyond my limited writing skills.

The Truth. At Last
****

I came back to the UK with a completely different perspective on life. I had seen, indeed had been blessed, and felt, what few of us ever have the opportunity to experience. For this I am truly thankful.

I had now come to the conclusion that I was going to remain single for evermore, maybe with the occasional girlfriend, but I was certain my mind that all I needed in my life was those that I loved and cared about.

I was never going to get into a long-term relationship again. This is something that I dare say a lot of us think after any relationship breakdown, but at that time I was sure in my own mind that this was the correct path to take.

I soon once again found employment with a driving school and went about the day to day running of such a business. I was once again seeing my children every two weeks and we all soon became accustomed to spending weekends together having a laugh and getting on with our lives.

No doubt, it was difficult without Susie being with me, she had been a huge part of not only my life, but also the children's, she had left an enormous hole that we were finding difficult to fill, but nonetheless we did our very best.

A year had gone past since myself and Susie separated. We spoke a few times on the phone, but these were rare occurrences indeed. More often than not any communication between myself and Susie was done through email. We both remained very polite and courteous. And at no time were there any arguments.

I did however ask her on one or two occasions whether she was still certain in her own mind that she wanted a formal separation and divorce in the future. Her mind had not changed, whilst I knew it hurt her to say it, she was still very much of the opinion that she wanted a divorce.

I had made up my mind that I would not push Susie into a

corner or question her motives for her decision. It was a decision she had come to through long and protracted thought, and hopefully in the future it would be the correct decision for her.

I was still heartbroken, but I realised that if Susie was to be happy then I had to keep this to myself and let her live the life that she thought was correct. I didn't want to upset or put any undue pressure on her to change her mind.

As I've said, we all make decisions in our lives in order that we may be happy, and I hoped, truly hoped, that the decision Susie had come to would be the correct decision for her, and she would one day find happiness.

Our lives, myself and the children's lives, were once again getting back to some sense of normality, if normality can be used to explain my life to date. However, the children were now 15 and 13 years old respectively, and they began to show signs of a slightly worrying nature.

They had hinted that things are at home were at times rather stressful, and I could see in their faces that there was some unhappiness somewhere in their lives.

They would not say any more other than 'Mum was tired, and exhausted'. I asked them exactly what they meant, but at no time would they expand on their opinion. It was rather a worrying time because I did not want to push the matter any further in case it upset not only the children, but Jennie also.

But after several more weeks I started to receive phone calls from my children that were rather worrying in nature. They told me that Steve was drinking 'again' and he had walked out of the house.

As you would imagine I was somewhat shocked and bemused at such a statement. We all like a drink now and again, or most of us do, but this sounded as if Steve really did have some degree of a problem with alcohol.

I took it upon myself to phone Jennie and ask her what was going on. She told me that yes, Steve did have a problem with drink, and indeed he was a recovering alcoholic, but everything was under control and there was no need to worry.

Not that it was any of my business, but I had never been told this before. For all I knew, Jennie, Steve, and the children were a relatively happy family unit, and for all intents and purposes, living a happy life.

To be told that the children's stepfather was a recovering alcoholic was indeed a shock to the system. After all, I had in the past talked with Steve, and he did not seem as if he had any great problems in his life. He always seemed calm, polite and understanding of any situation.

Over the next several weeks the phone calls from my children were becoming more and more frequent. I would often have my eldest daughter on the phone hysterical and telling me that Steve had yet again had a drink and had walked out of the house, or indeed wrecked the house.

I again questioned Jennie as to exactly what was going on. I did after all have my children's best interests at heart, and if I thought their lives were in anyway unhappy, I as the father, should know.

Jennie once again admitted that Steve was a recovering alcoholic, and as of late he had indeed been on the booze again. But, it was a situation that she could cope with and, she assured that the children would come to no harm.

It would have been easy for me to judge the situation, but I was no longer part of the family unit and I thought to judge such a situation would not only be unfair, but also very judgemental.

As time went by it was obvious from the phone calls I was from receiving my children that the situation at home was becoming untenable, one evening the situation at Jennies house became untenable in the extreme.

Jennie rang me and was hysterical in nature. She told me the barest of outlines of what had gone on. Steve had once again hit the bottle big time and he had been escorted from the house by the police. The children were also hysterical and you could hear them in the background sobbing their hearts out.

I made the decision to say to Jennie that if she wanted me to go to the house and help in anyway I could I was only too willing to do so. It was an evening that was to change the rest of my life, once again.

Looking Back
****

I arrived at Jennies house at what can only be described as a disaster zone. The house had been wrecked, and my family were for all intents and purposes totally confused and dazed.

I did my best to comfort the children and tell them everything would be OK, and I would sort it out as soon as possible. I told Jennie that I would do whatever I could to help them get through this difficult time, and nothing they asked of me would be too much of a problem.

Once I had the situation under some degree of control I decided that this was the time to be forthright with Jennie and ask her exactly what was going on. The answers I received to my questions were not only surprising, but horrifying.

It transpired that Steve, whilst being a recovering alcoholic had gone back on the booze on at least three occasions during their marriage. Each time the aftermath he left was one of devastation. He would often wreck the house, and worry little for anybody, or anything, apart from his next drink.

I am not about to judge an alcoholic, I have never been an alcoholic, I have known a few, but to say I have a complete understanding would be unfair.

It is a terrible, terrible, disease, and one that I would not wish on my worst enemy. But to be faced with such a scenario involving my own family was indeed a shock to the system.

I am a smoker after all, and I know only too well how difficult it is to give up smoking. I have tried on numerous occasions, and failed miserably each time. While this cannot compare to alcoholism I do have some idea of how difficult it might be to give up the dreaded booze.

Whilst all and sundry can pontificate and advise, it is only when the alcoholic in question decides to give up the drink that any form of acceptance can take place. I am not about to criticise or castigate Steve for the disease he had.

It later transpired that Steve had been given every

available means of help and counselling. Indeed, his mother had paid for him to be treated in an exclusive residential unit that dealt specifically with addiction in all its forms.

But this was to no avail, he had once again gone back on the booze and not only wrecked his life, but all those around him. I was by this time trying to get some degree of understanding on the matter, but it was extremely hard.

What transpired later was something that fills me with dread to this day. Jennie explained to me that on the several occasions I had heard certain rumours, and indeed when myself and Susie took care of my children for those three months, Jennie had been very ,very ill.

As the conversation went on it was obvious that I had through no fault of my own been unaware of the situation unfolding at Jennies house.

The conversation went on long into the evening and everything started to make sense. Jennie then informed me that just after the birth of our eldest daughter, Jane some fifteen years ago, she had been very unwell.

You will be only too aware that I was at this time also aware that Jennie, whilst not being ill, was definitely different. Unbeknown to me she had been diagnosed with schizophrenia and bipolar disorder, or to use layman's terms, manic depressive.

The schizophrenia had been diagnosed by her doctor a little after five weeks of the birth of our daughter, and the bipolar disorder had been diagnosed some two weeks later. I wish I could say that this now makes sense for the way Jennie had acted just after the birth of our daughter, but to try and make sense of this situation was more than I could possibly do.

I knew little of schizophrenia, and even less of bipolar disorder, and to say that I was at a loss as to what to say would be an understatement. I will not go into details of the two illnesses, suffice to say that they change the individual afflicted with them beyond all recognition.

To those of you who have never come across

schizophrenia or bipolar disorder before these terms can seem somewhat confusing. If I were to try and explain them it would be like this. That both disorders are for all intents and purposes are incurable, they can however be controlled to some extent with drugs.

I have since being told of Jennies illnesses read every book, every article, every webpage concerning the disorders mentioned, and to this day I am falling far short of understanding them to any great degree.

Schizophrenia and bipolar disorder not only change the person afflicted radically, but they also impact greatly on all those around them. I could at this point harp back to my marriage with Jennie and explain once again, or try to explain once again, the atmosphere we were living in.

Jennie at that time had become a person that was unrecognisable to me and all those around her, but at no point in time did I or anyone else ever think that the change in her was due to the illnesses involved.

All I knew at the time was that Jennie had changed radically, and did not want me in her life any more. I will not explain yet again our history, as I have done this in previous chapters, but to say that the disorder affected all our lives is an understatement.

Schizophrenia and bipolar disorder make the afflicted act so differently that until you have experienced it, it is very difficult to envisage. The person involved becomes unrecognisable to all those around them, and their actions are actions that once upon a time they would have never taken.

I was still trying as best I could to comprehend the situation and assimilate the information that had been given to me, but at this stage I was exhausted and tired and in truth I could not begin to imagine what had taken place.

I left Jennie that evening full of emotions that were as confusing then as they are now. All I knew was that at a certain point in her life these illnesses had taken such a hold on her that any degree of normality in her life was never going to take place.

Several days went past and I was doing all I could to help the situation at Jennies house. I did my best to comfort my children, and in no small measure comfort Jennie and tell her that everything would be alright, and anything they asked me would not be a problem, I would do all I could to help them get through this difficult time.

My one overriding question to Jennie was simply this, why the hell hadn't she told me that she had been diagnosed with schizophrenia and bipolar disorder? Surely if she had done so we could have found help and maybe, we could have built a future together?

To this day she finds it difficult to explain to me, but she often says to me that at that point in her life, because of the illnesses, she felt as if she could not speak to anyone, she felt a failure, and for all intents and purposes very, very alone.

I told her that all she had to do was to have told me and we could have worked through the situation. At that time all I saw was the woman I love change overnight, and I could not understand why. I thought it was my fault, Australia's fault, in fact, not once did it cross my mind that there was a far more sinister reason for the way Jennie was acting.

All Jennie could do was to apologise to me and say that she regretted with all her heart the day she asked me to move out of the family home. She said that while she had regretted her decision it was a decision that she had to live with, no matter what.

She also explained to me that whilst her and Steve's marriage was at times very good, there were times when the marriage was a disaster zone. As I said, I am not about to judge Steve, but when he did go back on the booze it affected not only him, but his family hugely.

Combine Steve's alcoholism with Jennies illnesses and you have in no small measure a powder keg ready to go off. When Steve did go back on the bottle it was all Jennie could do to hold the family together, at times this was too much, and it was then that the family disintegrated.

Steve's alcoholism not only impacted on his life catastrophically, but also on Jennies and the children's. Once again I asked why on earth hadn't someone told me? All Jennie would say that she saw me and Susie as extremely happy, and if she had told me, what on earth was I going to do?

I explained to her that even though I was extremely happy with Susie I still would have done all I possibly could for the family. After all, Susie would have understood completely, and wouldn't have minded in the least that I was trying to help.

I have since broached the subject of the way the separation and divorce were handled. Jennie has told me that she had no control whatsoever in the separation and divorce, it was in actual fact taken out of her hands completely and dealt with by other people.

I believe to this day that the people involved did what they did, and said what they said with the best possible intentions. They had after all been made aware of Jennies illnesses, and I dare say their actions were thought at the time to be the best possible for Jennie. They knew only too well that Jennies mental state at the time was extremely fragile, and they would do anything to protect her.

So in reality, even though I still feel aggrieved at some of the actions taken, I guess I can come somewhere near understanding their reasons for acting in such a way. I cannot excuse, or forgive their actions, and what they tried to do to me, but I can understand very slightly why they chose to take such a path.

Trying To Understand
****

By this time several weeks had past and I was trying to comprehend the situation I now found myself in. We can all at times look back at our lives and wish we had done things differently, but I have learned through bitter experience that this is foolish, you can only deal with the present situation you find yourself in, and act accordingly.

The discussions between myself and Jennie were at times very emotional and heart wrenching, but in a very small way I did manage to clarify some points that I had been confused about.

To say I have a complete understanding of what went on between myself and Jennie during our marriage would be an over exaggeration, but I can now see that the actions she and her family took were understandable.

Schizophrenia and bipolar as I have said, have a massive impact on not only affected, but all they come into contact with. I could quite easily accuse, castigate and blame Jennie for what went on, but this would be with hindsight.

If truth were known, at times I still resent the way she acted, what she and her family did to me, but then I come to the realisation that Jennie in particular, never said or did anything out of spite or cruelty.

Schizophrenia and bipolar disorder are to blame to a far greater extent. Yes, it would be easy of me and others to say that Jennie could of acted differently. But with the understanding I now have of these disorders I can see that she had little choice in the matter.

I have said previously that I have read every article concerning the aforementioned illnesses, and I can honestly say that if Jennie had not been afflicted with these these illnesses then she would acted wholly differently. She would in actual fact of been the person I first met.

And to some extent I still cannot understand her reasoning for not telling me when she was diagnosed with these illnesses.

There again, I am coming at this from a completely logical viewpoint. When these two dreadful illnesses take hold, logic exists no more, and it is all the afflicted can do to at times, carry on with their lives.

Jennie never purposely went out a way to hurt or destroy me, and her family I guess in the long run never did so either. Their main concern was for Jennie and the children, For that I cannot blame them.

I would like you to remember one thing. Up to around thirty years ago those afflicted with schizophrenia and/or bipolar disorder were simply looked upon as being 'mad'. It was as plain and simple as that. Anyone with these diseases were to some extent, castigated and completely misunderstood.

They were often placed in mental institutions and the authorities did their level best to help and 'cure' them. Unlike today, these diseases were looked upon by the vast majority of us with both distrust, and skepticism.

And even today the poor unfortunates afflicted with either of these illnesses are still looked upon as 'freaks' by the majority of people. The illnesses are so misunderstood that it truly does begger belief.

Be honest, the only time the vast majority of us hear, or see the word 'schizophrenia' is when we see or hear a report on TV or in the papers. More often than not the report unfortunately says that a 'paranoid schizophrenic' has yet again maimed or killed some poor innocent victim.

Admittedly, these are not everyday occurrences, but they do happen, and when they do most peoples reaction is to say, 'Why on earth are these 'types' of people allowed to wander the streets'? Or, 'They should all be locked up, and the key thrown away'.

We have little understanding of what is going on, or indeed the truth. That is not to apportion blame to anyone of us. After all, as I have said throughout this book, until we experience anything 'first hand' it is very difficult to understand what is happening, even to the smallest degree.

The illnesses concerned whilst being terrible and catastrophic are still to some extent completely misunderstood by the vast majority of us. I am in no way exonerating or indeed excusing the actions of the afflicted when these actions result in, at times death. But what I have come to realise is that those who have these illnesses act in a way that the vast majority of us find totally repellant and inexcusable.

I was too of this mindset many months ago. I have now come to realise that these people need help so drastically. There is a misconception that the schizophrenic involved was acting out of malice and sheer evil.

When in truth they had little, or no control over what they were doing. It is more the case that the 'system' we have in place in this country has often let them down. But more importantly, let the innocent victims of the murder or assault down so devastatingly.

Please try to understand. I am in no way trying to excuse certain behaviours that we all hear and see about daily. There are many reports day after day that yet again inform us that yet another murder, stabbing, rape, has taken place. To say that the perpetrators of these crimes were all schizophrenic would be an injustice.

More often than not the crimes committed are by those that are just ordinary scum. People who think little about what they have done. People who could not care less about the pain and grief they are inflicting not only on their victims, but also the family and friends of the innocent victims. If these people can be bought to justice then I agree wholeheartedly that the remainder of their lives should be one of punishment and incarceration.

But if it can be 'proved' that a crime was committed by an individual who suffered from a terrible mental disease then these people should be cared for by the 'system' if at all possible.

If they are going to be a danger to the general public for the foreseeable future then they should be kept away from the general public until they are either deemed 'safe' or sadly, if they are incurable and a danger to the public then we have little choice but to keep them secure in a form of establishment.

I hope I have been able to convey what I am trying to say. After all, I am a former prison officer. I am not what could be called a 'liberal do-gooder'. I know only too well that the vast majority of violent crime is committed by those that are perfectly sane and they knew exactly what they were doing. At times imprisonment is too good for these people, that is as much as I will say.

Having said all of this, Jennie is fortunately not a 'paranoid' schizophrenic. Her illness means that whilst she may still suffer from some of the same feelings as a 'paranoid', she has none of the violent behaviour that is inherent with the paranoid part of the illness.

More often than not her behaviour is one of depression and loneliness. The only harm she is, or rather was going to do, would be to herself. Which is a sphere of schizophrenia that whilst not as bad as other spheres, still comes as a shock to the uninitiated.

I hope I have managed to clarify what I am trying to say. I feel I have fallen somewhat short, if so I apologise. I am not a medical expert, just a middle aged bloke that is doing his level best to cope, help, and hopefully explain to 'laymen' what terrible diseases schizophrenia and bipolar disorder are.

Learning Once Again
****

Some months later I moved into Jennies, it wasn't an action I took lightly. There were many conversations that took place between all of us before such a conclusion was arrived at. I would love to say that it has been an easy transition for not only myself, but also Jennie and the children. But nothing could be further from the truth. Jennies mindset for the first three or four months that I went to live with them was one of blame, and guilt.

It is only through time, understanding and love that we have now come to a place in the lives that whilst not being perfect, is far better.

The situation with Steve was not only a truly devastating period of Jennies life, but it affected everyone who came into contact with them.

I could at this point blame Jennie for choosing such a man, but as I have said, it is all too easy to look back in hindsight and wish we had done things differently.

She did what she thought was right at the time, and I am not going to blame her for this. Yes, I agree that to the bystander her actions and emotions can come across as callous, but until you have an understanding on a very personal level then to judge would not only be unfair, but also extremely naïve.

So, officially we are now living back once again as man and wife, I am now a 'husband' and loving dad. My children, though we still squabble and fight as in any ordinary family, call me once again 'dad', and the love that show me is indescribable.

The last year in my life has been an enormous upheaval, totally confusing, and at times I felt as if I had no one to turn to. But now, I find myself in a place that I once was. If the truth were known Jennie is a completely different person, the illnesses she suffers from make her into such a person.

Occasionally there is a glimpse of the old Jennie that I used to know before the illnesses took hold, but this is only a fleeting glance. The vast majority of the time she is a person that I have to learn to love and respect again.

It hasn't been easy, at times I've wanted to blame her for what went on. But there is little point in taking such an avenue, because quite simply, she is a wholly different person. It would be no use me trying to blame this 'new' person for the way she acted.

The Jennie I once knew many, many, years ago has gone, and has been replaced by someone that is taking time to get to know. It's not easy, but it is a journey that I am only too willing to take.

We all make mistakes in life, some we are fully conscious of, some we are not. I know only too well that the mistakes I've made in the past have hurt many people, all I can do now is try to get my family back to where it should be.

It is going to take a long, long, time to get any degree of 'normality' back into our lives. There are many reasons for this. I have to learn to build a new life with a woman that bears little resemblance to the woman I once knew many years ago.

I also have to accept the fact that for the vast majority of time my children grew up without me in their lives. To them, as much as they are to me, we are all different, and we are learning to accept each others habits, both good and bad.

And if I said Jennies illnesses do not affect us all I would be lying. The illnesses she has dictate how myself and Jennie live our lives. To a certain degree the illnesses also affect the children, but I am doing my best to make sure that they are still 'children' and in as much, should act as children.

They should be going out with their mates, having sleepovers, laughing and joking. They have seen enough in their young lives to last a lifetime. Now it is my responsibility to make sure the lives they lead are as carefree and as fun filled as possible, I think I am succeeding.

Jennie is now in a better place, however this has only come about because of the effort and work that has been put in by myself. There have been many arguments and disagreements, but we have worked through this and we can now see light at the end of the tunnel.

Her routine before was one of abject misery. The vast majority of the time she would spend most of the day in bed, not talking to a soul. I admit that a lot of this behaviour is part of the 'package' of schizophrenia and bipolar, but a lot of the blame has to be laid squarely at the medication she was taking.

Within four months I had several meetings with her medical team and we came to the conclusion that Jennies medication was to blame for the 'life' Jennie was leading.

Thankfully now the new medication she is on has helped massively. Yes, she still has her bad days when all she wants to do is hide away, or blame herself for everything. But for the vast majority of days she is energetic, full of life, and most importantly, can see that there is now a point in living.

With patience, love, and understanding I am sure that we will all get to the point in our lives where we can say they are 'ordinary'. All I can do is try my best. There will be happiness and heartbreak along the way, but that after all, is life.

Recovery
****

One of the many steps on the road to recovery was to go to Australia as a family unit. So in August of 2009, myself, Jennie, and the children all went to Queensland for a month's holiday.

To say that we all enjoyed our time immensely does not come anywhere near describing the feelings and emotions we all had. Even though my children didn't remember most of what they saw, they still saw that Australia was indeed a wonderful country.

But, more importantly was Jennies reaction to seeing Australia once again. For the vast majority of time she was relaxed, happy and contented. I think she now has an understanding of what Australia did for me in my darkest hours. She can see the country and its people really were my salvation, and I think she is thankful for that.

Because of the disorders she suffers from, her memory at times can be severely impaired. But once we arrived in Cairns the joy and happiness that was etched into her face was a wonder to behold, and to see her smile and be happy in a country that once she knew well, is a memory that I will hold dear.

We did all the normal 'touristy' things, spent too much money, ate too much, sunbathed too much, but to see the look on Jennies face when we pulled up at our 'old' Edmonton house was worth every penny, calorie, and burn.

If only she had told me of her illnesses before, we may of still been living in the house we were now parked outside of. But that is to live in cloud cuckoo land, to think such thoughts is foolish. But, that doesn't stop me from having such thoughts.

Australia and its people will always be somewhere that I can call 'home'. The acceptance and welcoming embrace of the country, and its people will always be part of me. And hopefully one day, my families.

So there you have it, it's not my whole life story, and I have left certain aspects out as to not offend or upset any individual. But I hope in some small measure that this book goes to show what Australia means to me as an individual. At times it has been my very best friend, it has been there through some of the worst times of my life, and I know it will always will be there.

I could in no small measure blame Australia for some of the experiences I have had, but once again, hindsight is a wonderful thing. When looked at in more depth I have come to realise that Australia has, good and bad, been my salvation.

I now find myself in a place that I am trying to make sense of. I am a citizen of Australia, and by birth my youngest daughter is also a citizen. My eldest daughter would be allowed into Australia without any problems because of my citizenship status, hopefully.

But, if Australia is to play any significant part in our future lives then Jennies medical conditions will have to be taken into consideration. I'll not go into the details about how the immigration authorities look upon any application that we may make in future for residency, suffice to say that the criteria laid down can be very strict and comprehensive.

I have no idea if we will ever live permanently in Australia once again. That is down to the relevant authorities when we finally decide to make an application. I have spoken to several migration agents that have said there may be some issues, I have also spoken to several migration agents who believe that now that Jennies illnesses are well under control, and for the most part she is a lot better, then the immigration authorities would allow Jennie in.

Myself and Jennie have spoken about our future lives, and we both agree that we would truly love to live in Australia once again. It was a place that Jennie loved, and one she has happy memories of.

There is still an awful lot to sort out in the UK, and you could say the next few months are going to be extremely difficult. But we are adamant in the fact that one day we will return to Australia to live permanently.

If however the authorities do not allow Jennie to once

again settle in Australia I know in my heart of hearts that Australia will always be part of me. Whether we go back on a regular basis, if finances allow of course, then so be it.

My family of course will always come first, and if this means us remaining in the UK for the foreseeable future, or even for the rest of our lives, then that is fine with me. I have learnt over the years that those around you are the most important things in life, and I will do all I can to make all those around me happy.

It would be no use to me saying that Australia will not play a significant part in me and my families future life. No matter how small or insignificant its role, I can assure you that Australia and its people will always be part of our lives no matter where we find ourselves.

All I can do at this moment in time is look back at my life and realise that everything that happened, happened for a reason. I may not have understood the reasons at the time, but I can now look back upon those times with hindsight, and come to realise that every experience, both good and horrific, were there for a reason.

Conclusion. Well Nearly
****

Well, I hope you have enjoyed reading my story. I must admit that at times it was not an easy story to relate to you. As I said in the introduction, it has been somewhat of a cathartic experience for me, and I hope that in some small measure it has shown you just what my relationship with Australia has been over these many years.

It is a place where at times I found comfort when I could find comfort nowhere else. The vast majority of the time this was through my own fault, and nobody else's.

As you would have gathered through reading this book, I at times, can be one of the most unreasonable and selfish people on God's green earth, so therefore it is only right and proper that at certain times in my life people around me chose to distance themselves somewhat, and try to make happier lives for themselves without me in them.

You could argue that certain things happen in life that are out of our control, but in reality, 'most' things in life are in our control, and it is irresponsible to say that this is not the case.

I therefore have paid the price on many occasions for being the type of person I am. I am not perfect, I don't know of anyone that is, if we were all perfect our lives would I imagine, be somewhat boring. But some of my actions in the past, and I dare say in the future, will impact on all those around me greatly, there is no way I can ever compensate for this.

So in essence all I am saying is this. I attach no blame to anyone else for the often disastrous situations I found myself in, it was as a consequence of my actions that I often found myself in a place that I would not wish on my worst enemy.

But each and every time Australia showed me that there was somewhere that would accept me for the way I was and am, both good and bad. She openly embraced me, and comforted me in a way that enabled me to carry on with my life when I thought that life itself was not worth carrying on with.

Those of you lucky enough, or fortunate enough, to have lived a life that is fairly, and I hate to use this word, 'normal', then I applaud you. Maybe you as a person have had the good fortune to have around you a group of people who love you dearly, and stay with you.

I wish I could say the same, but unfortunately because of my actions some of the people that I loved and cared about with all my heart decided that they could take no more, and had to call it a day when I kept on acting very unreasonably.

I bear absolutely no malice or hate toward these people, because they in the long run had to live a life that was to some extent happy and fulfilling, and if this meant me not being in their lives because of the way I had acted, then I accept full responsibility for this.

People and places change all the time, this is part of being human, and to think otherwise would be foolhardy. But Australia has never turned away from me, and not accepted me. That makes it sound as if I am apportioning blame to the people who decided that they could take no more of me, nothing could be further from the truth.

All they did was to realise that if I was still in their lives, then their own lives would be to some extent, be unhappy. As I said, I hold no malice or apportion blame whatsoever. But Australia, even though at times had every right to turn her back on me, has never done so.

I keep calling Australia 'she' and I've done my best to explain just why I use this terminology. In essence Australia is in my eyes, a female.

As with most females, and may I add, the vast majority of females have always shown themselves to be honest and loving, Australia showed me love, warmth, compassion and absolute joy. But at other times she showed me anger, hate, and distain. Her personality is made up of many different facets, some positive, some negative.

But I accept wholeheartedly these many different aspects

of her personality. Maybe, just maybe, if I had accepted earlier in my life these same characteristics in my human relationships then my life would have been totally different.

I have no way of knowing this. To try and imagine my life any differently is foolhardy. But all I can say in my defence is this. That I never, ever, went out of my way to hurt those around me. I never intentioned to upset or annoy anyone. I realise that we can all act in a way that at times can seem somewhat 'selfish'.

To try and erase these actions is impossible. We can all live with regret and sorrow, but we can in equal measure, acknowledge the love and compassion we also showed the people in our lives, and indeed, were shown. We can all learn from this. Or rather I hope we can.

A Child's Story. Explanation
****

The story related to you in the prelude is in actual fact my story. It actually happened in the summer of 1971. I spent many a happy holiday with my grandparents during my summer holidays away from school.

I had always been fascinated by the sea and what it contained. I would pester 'nan' and 'pop' constantly to take me to the beach. They never once said no, that's just the type of people they were, loving grandparents.

To have had them in my life, though this time was far too short, was an experience that I am eternally grateful for. Thanks nan and pop for everything you did for me. I dare say that you are looking down at me right now and just coming to realise what this day meant to me.

I don't think you knew what just happened that day. What we all shared that day, though unbeknown to you, was an event that was to a certain degree, to change the course of my life. Thanks for taking me to the beach that day, thank you so very much.

That day I found the 'boomerang' was special. In truth I have no idea where this boomerang had come from. It was later explained to me that a boomerang was something that the aboriginal people used for hunting, and it came from Australia.

At the time this explanation meant little to me. But as I have got older I have come to realise what it may of meant. I am a fully grown adult, and in as much should be reasoned and logical in all my actions and thoughts. I at times fall well short of acting in such a way, but I do my best.

The boomerang in question has pride of place on the living room wall. Nearly forty years after me finding this boomerang it is still with me.

I look at it each and everyday with wonder and excitement. I truly believe that the boomerang to this day was found by that eight year old boy, who I barely recognise now, for a reason.

I honestly believe that it was 'sent' to me for a reason. That it came over on the ocean currents all the way from Australia, and found an innocent eight year old who didn't realise the impact it was to have.

It travelled some ten thousand miles, maybe more, to be with a boy who was looking for a purpose in life. He may not of realised he wanted a purpose, after all, he was only eight years old, innocent, and not at all interested in anything other than having fun.

It is true that the boomerang may have been purchased in the UK, and some poor hapless individual had lost it hours or days before. But in all honesty, at that time, in 1971, there were very few boomerangs mass marketed in this country.

Few people even knew what a boomerang was. So to think that its journey was instigated in this country is somewhat unbelievable. I honestly think to this day that it had indeed travelled those many of thousands of miles. After all, it was not, and is not, in the best of conditions.

Battered, worn, slightly skewed in the wrong direction is a very apt description of the boomerang in its present state. It looks for all intense and purposes as if it has travelled many thousands of miles.

I have researched and investigated the whole matter of boomerangs since that time. My main reason for taking such a path is simply to find out if indeed boomerangs were ever manufactured in this country. And upon further investigation I have found a very small maker of boomerangs in Scotland that have been in business since the early seventies.

But they make and sell a very specific make of boomerang, nothing at all like the one I found. The only reference to my boomerang is to a company that is still in business on the east coast of Australia that manufacture the exact same boomerang that I have presently on the living room wall.

So I am left with two conclusions. Either the boomerang

was brought back to the UK by a holiday maker from Australia and lost somewhere in this country, most likely a beach.

Or it found its place in this country because it was originally made, and used in Australia. For some reason it found itself on the ocean currents, and found its way into a young eight year olds boys hands where he excitedly picked it up to show his grandparents.

I know which one I believe, but I will allow you to come to your own conclusion.

I realise that to many thousands of you what I am saying will be dismissed as wishful thinking. I cannot blame you in the slightest for this. I would of done the same thing many years ago.

But I can honestly say that for some reason, however inexplicable, this boomerang found an eight year old boy one hot summer's day on a beach on the other side of the world. It found a boy who's future would be written from that day on.

Daydreaming, wishful thinking, completely ridiculous, maybe. But to this now fully grown adult there is only one conclusion to come to. And I will not deviate from this thought process, however tenuous the link.

A Final Note
****

The title of this book is 'The Long Road Home'. After having read this book I will leave it to your own interpreatation as to whether I have indeed arrived 'home'.

Is my journey complete, or does is still have someway to go? I have after all, come full circle, and the place that I now find myself in is a place that I would never of imagined several months ago.

As I said, I will leave it down to you as, (hopefully) unbiased individuals to be the judge. Who knows what will happen next? I for one will not comment, or rather, cannot comment. I have learnt that to try and second guess the future is not only foolhardy, but it is also impossible to predict.

Whichever path my life goes down from here on in I know it will be filled with love, compassion, understanding, adventure, upset, worry and stress. These are after all, integral to our very existence. They are indeed facets of our very being that make us 'human'.

I truly have no idea which path my life will take. All I know is that whichever path it takes I am to some extent in 'control' of such a path.

But, I am also aware that this path will ultimately be influenced by all those around me, sometimes for the better, sometimes for the worse.

So to try and second guess what the future holds is foolhardy. All I know is that I have lived a life that is far from ordinary. At times I wish I had lived a life that was indeed 'ordinary'. But there again, would I be the person I am today if I had done so?

This book is in no way as comprehensive as I would of initially liked it to have been. Time, and to a certain extent resources, have negated such an avenue been taken. For this reason there are many experiences that I had to leave out in order for my story to be written. Maybe one day I will find the time to chronicle such experiences. Some of these experiences are not easy to write about. Some truly awful, some surprising, and many that are funny.

As I have said, my life has not been ordinary, far from it. One day I would like the experiences I have had to be written about in detail, and maybe only when this is done can you as a reader truly have a clearer picture of what sort of life I have had. Maybe one day I will get around to writing such a book.

More importantly than these experiences are the people I have met along the way. You have all had a massive impact upon my life and I thank you all for that.

I apologise for not being able to include the impact you had on me, so I have included at the end of this book some the names of the people I have met along the way. I hope in the very slightest of ways that this repays your love, kindness, and compassion you showed during my journey.

I realise that in comparison to a lot of peoples lives my life has been blessed. There are stories out there of absolute sadness and grief. I cannot compare my life at all to your very own. But I hope in some small way I have been able to show you that even though at times our lives can seem so out of control, there is more often than not a light at the end of the tunnel.

If there is no such light then my heart goes out to you, and I can assure you that you are in my prayers. I have no idea where these prayers go, a God, higher being, an entity, or maybe they just disperse into the atmosphere, I have my own ideas born out of experience. But wherever they go, I will still pray for you.

I often thank my lucky stars that I have led the life I have. For all its ups and downs, it has been a life that has shown me what is truly important in life. And for that I am eternally grateful.

When all is said and done I hope you have enjoyed reading my story, and in some small way, I hope you have found it entertaining. Thank you.

With grateful thanks to the following people.

Jo, Palm Cove. Thank you so much for the support and friendship you showed me when I first arrived. I will never be able to repay the debt I owe you, it is to big to comprehend.

William. Johannesburg. Thanks for stepping in, when in reality you had no good reason to do so.

Brian. Sydney. Thanks for the time you took to make sure I got back.

Steve. Sandfire Roadhouse. Thanks for the lift mate. You said I should have never bought the 'Skip on Wheels'.

Mel & Teresa. Somewhere Outback. Thanks for sharing a very special moment, and thanks for the advice. I constantly think about what you said.

Freddo. Perth. Told you I would do it.

Gavin. Monkey Mia. I lent you that fishing rod in good faith mate. Where is it?

Stu, Toni, and the Littlen's. Karratha. To have the warmth of a family around me that week was an inspiration. Thank you so much.

Brian. Somewhere in Perth. I hope you found what you were looking for. You deserve it.

Gary & Fiona. Bali. The 'Ship' will never be the same again!

Julie & dog, 'Rocky'. Green Island. You made me laugh all evening. By the way Julie, I haven't forgotton I owe you $20. Give him a pat for me.

Printed in Great Britain by
Amazon.co.uk, Ltd.,
Marston Gate.